302·542

A-LEVEL YEAR 2

STUDENT GUIDE

AQA

Sociology

Crime and deviance
(with theory and methods)

Dave O'Leary

Series editor: Joan Garrod

Acknowledgement: The author would like to thank the sociology students at Kingsthorpe College, particularly Maddie Wanford and Kahvan Bryan, for their support.

Philip Allan, an imprint of Hodder Education, an Hachette UK company, Blenheim Court, George Street, Banbury, Oxfordshire OX16 5BH

Orders

Bookpoint Ltd, 130 Park Drive, Milton Park, Abingdon, Oxfordshire OX14 4SB

tel: 01235 827827

fax: 01235 400401

e-mail: education@bookpoint.co.uk

Lines are open 9.00 a.m.–5.00 p.m., Monday to Saturday, with a 24-hour message answering service. You can also order through the Hodder Education website: www.hoddereducation.co.uk

© Dave O'Leary 2016

ISBN 978-1-4718-5682-2

First printed 2016

Impression number 5 4 3 2

Year 2020 2019 2018 2017

This Guide has been written specifically to support students preparing for the AQA A-level Sociology examinations. The content has been neither approved nor endorsed by AQA and remains the sole responsibility of the author.

Cover photo: Marco Govel/Fotolia

Typeset by Integra Software Services Pvt. Ltd., Pondicherry, India

Printed in Italy

Hachette UK's policy is to use papers that are natural, renewable and recyclable products and made from wood grown in sustainable forests. The logging and manufacturing processes are expected to conform to the environmental regulations of the country of origin.

Contents

Content Guidance

Crime and deviance

Theory and methods

Questions & Answers

■ Getting the most from this book

Exam tips

Advice on key points in the text to help you learn and recall content, avoid pitfalls, and polish your exam technique in order to boost your grade.

Knowledge check

Rapid-fire questions throughout the Content Guidance section to check your understanding.

Knowledge check answers

1 Turn to the back of the book for the Knowledge check answers.

Summaries

- Each core topic is rounded off by a bullet-list summary for quick-check reference of what you need to know.

Exam-style questions

Commentary on the questions

Tips on what you need to do to gain full marks, indicated by the icon **e**

Sample student answers

Practise the questions, then look at the student answers that follow.

Commentary on sample student answers

Read the comments (preceded by the icon **e**) showing how many marks each answer would be awarded in the exam and exactly where marks are gained or lost.

■About this book

This guide is for students following the AQA A-level Sociology course. It deals with the topic of crime and deviance with theory and methods.

There are two main sections to this guide:

■ **Content Guidance** — this provides details of the topics of crime and deviance and sociological theory. There is also a section examining the link between theory and sociological methods. Topic areas on crime and theory examine key ideas, and arguments, stating the main points of evaluation and include the key concepts and key thinkers. The defined words are key words for this specification.

■ **Questions and Answers** — this shows you the kind of questions you can expect in the A-level Paper 3 examination. The first two test papers are followed by two sample answers, Student A (A*-grade response) and Student B (C-grade response). Test papers 3 and 4 each consist of a practice A-level Paper 3 for you to attempt yourself with guidance on how to answer.

How to use this guide

When you study crime and deviance topics and theory and methods in class, read the corresponding information from the Content Guidance sections to become familiar with the topic. You should use these sections to complete your own revision notes, for example on each method and topic within crime and deviance. You should then complete Test paper 1 or 2. It is advisable to focus on questions on one topic area, method etc. at a time. After you have completed your own answers you should compare them with the answers from Students A and B. These and the examiner's comments that follow them can be used to amend your revision notes.

The A-level specification is shown in detail on the AQA website: www.aqa.org.uk/7192. Follow the links to Sociology A-level (7192).

Content Guidance

This section outlines the major issues and themes of **Crime and deviance** and **Theory and methods**.

The content of **Crime and deviance** falls into the following areas:

- Crime, deviance, social order and social control
- The social distribution of crime and deviance by ethnicity, gender and social class, including recent patterns and trends in crime
- Globalisation and crime in contemporary society; the media and crime; green crime; human rights and state crimes
- Crime control, surveillance, prevention and punishment, victims, and the role of the criminal justice system and other agencies

The content of **Theory and methods** falls into following areas:

- Consensus, conflict, structural and social action theories
- The concepts of modernity and postmodernity in relation to sociological theory
- The nature of science and the extent to which sociology can be regarded as scientific
- The relationship between theory and methods
- Debates about subjectivity, objectivity and value freedom
- The relationship between sociology and social policy

Note that sociological methods, which you will have studied in Year 1, are covered in Student Guide 1.

Crime and deviance

■ Sociological theories of crime and deviance

Functionalism, strain and subcultural theories

- Durkheim (1897) believed that crime was inevitable and would be an increasing problem in modern society as rapid social change and diversity could potentially result in anomie. However, he felt that a certain level of crime was a normal part of a healthy society and would lead to various positive functions such as allowing positive social change to occur and acting as a **safety valve** to prevent more serious crime. The criminal justice system and punishment also have the function of reminding people of the boundaries of acceptable behaviour and promoting social solidarity through reaffirming shared values.

- However, Durkheim's theory has been criticised for focusing on social control and conformity rather than explaining why some groups commit more crime than others. Merton (1938) developed a functionalist explanation of crime and deviance and acknowledged that crime could be **dysfunctional** for society. He argues that deviance occurs as a result of the strain between socially accepted goals such as achieving material success (the American dream) and socially approved ways of achieving these goals such as hard work in school and the workplace.

- Merton argues that in the USA the main cultural goal is the American dream but that, despite notions of meritocracy, some sections of society lack the **legitimate opportunity structures** to achieve this goal. This would create anomie for individuals who were excluded from institutional means and would result in crime and deviance.

Anomie A feeling of normlessness. Crime and deviance are likely to occur when people are unsure about or are less committed to shared values and rules.

Exam tip

Be prepared to link basic functionalist concepts and arguments to their explanation of crime and deviance. As a structural, consensus theory, functionalism argues that crime occurs when social solidarity is threatened by a lack of effective social control mechanisms and when institutions such as the family are failing to socialise people into a shared culture.

Utilitarian crime Crime committed for financial gain.

Table 1 The strain to anomie — Merton's goals-and-means scheme

Response	Goals	Means	Example	Likely social group
Conformity	Yes	Yes	University educated professional	Middle class
Innovation	Yes	No	Organised crime gang member or petty thief. Commits utilitarian crime	Working class (due to inadequate socialisation)
Ritualism	No	Yes	Routine office worker who follows the rules but has no interest in promotion or a career	Lower middle class (may have been over-socialised to conform)
Retreatism	No	No	Dropouts of society	Addicts, 'tramps' etc.
Rebellion	Different goals	Different means	Want to create a new 'social order'	Political radicals and revolutionaries

Crime and deviance

- **Subcultural** theories of A. Cohen and Cloward and Ohlin — these developed Merton's notion of **strain** and agree that the lack of **opportunity structures** can be used to explain working-class crime and deviance.
- A. Cohen argues that working-class boys would value success goals initially but failure in school due to a lack of legitimate opportunity structures would lead to status frustration. As a result of this frustration the boys collectively inverted and replaced middle-class values of educational success with alternative goals and ways of achieving status, such as truanting.
- Cloward and Ohlin identify three working-class subcultures that result from varying degrees of access to illegitimate opportunity structures:
  - **Criminal** Have access to illegitimate opportunity structures and utilitarian crime as they are socialised into a 'life of crime' by members of organised criminal gangs
  - **Conflict** Have little access to illegitimate opportunity structures due to a lack of organised crime gangs in their area but can achieve status through gang violence
  - **Retreatists** Have no access to either legitimate or illegitimate opportunity structures. They may have failed in the other two types of subculture and 'retreat' into a world of drugs.
- Miller argues that working-class men were deviant because of their distinctive culture. He argues that lower-working-class culture is characterised by focal concerns, which act as a release from the boredom of their lives and mean that they will inevitably be involved in criminal and deviant activities. For example, the focal concern of 'toughness' will lead to crime such as fighting while 'excitement' will lead to crimes such as joyriding.

> **Status frustration** When people are dissatisfied with their position in society.
>
> **Illegitimate opportunity structures** Illegal means of achieving success such as being in a gang and committing crimes such as theft.
>
> **Focal concerns** The main things that are valued in a culture.

Table 2 Comparison of Merton and subcultural theory

Agree with Merton	Disagree with Merton
Merton and subcultural strain theories of Cohen and Cloward and Ohlin argue that the working classes initially share mainstream values of success	Miller's version of subcultural theory states that lower-class culture is separate from mainstream values. It does not share the middle-class goal of the 'American dream'
Merton and subcultural strain theories argue that crime is higher among the working class as they have less access to legitimate opportunity structures such as good education	Cohen and Cloward and Ohlin argue that the working class adopt a collective, not individual, response to strain by joining a subculture
Working-class crime is often caused by the need for financial gain. Merton's innovator is similar to Cloward and Ohlin's criminal subculture, who may commit utilitarian crimes such as burglary	Crime can also be non-utilitarian. Cohen's subculture gained status from truanting and vandalising school property. Cloward and Ohlin's conflict subcultures earned status through winning 'turf wars'
Deviants might 'drop out' of society such as Merton's retreatism response and Cloward and Ohlin's retreatist subculture, whose cultural values may both focus around drug use	Cloward and Ohlin's retreatist subculture are 'double failures' as they lack access to illegitimate (criminal and conflict subcultures) as well as legitimate opportunity structures

Exam tip

To develop analysis, compare Merton's strain theory and subcultural theories with the left realists Lea and Young's version of subculture (see Table 3). While they have different views on the causes, both believe that subcultures may be unable to achieve society's cultural goals due to blocked opportunity structures.

Interactionist Matza (1971) rejects Miller and argues that rather than there being a distinctive subculture, groups in society use a set of deviant '**subterranean values**' that exist below mainstream values. People would normally keep these values under control but they would occasionally emerge in situations such as after drinking too much at the office party or the end of Year 13 holiday in Ibiza. Matza argues that when this occurs we use **techniques of neutralisation** (sets of excuses) to justify our deviant actions such as the 'denial of responsibility': 'That wasn't me, I was drunk'.

Evaluation

- **Merton** Are there just five types of adaptation and common goals in society? The American dream may not be applicable to the UK today.
- **A. Cohen** Are working-class deviants aware that they are 'inverting' middle-class values? Delinquent behaviour such as truanting may be done just 'for a laugh'.
- **Cloward and Ohlin** There may be more than three types of subculture and an individual may be involved in more than one, such as a small-time drug dealer who is also a user.
- **Miller** There is little evidence to suggest that focal concerns are restricted to working-class males. Does a completely separate, homogeneous working-class subculture exist? However, **New Right** sociologists such as Murray (1990) would support Miller's ideas, arguing that there is now a distinct **underclass** whose values encourage deviant and criminal behaviour.
- **Interactionists** such as Matza argue that separate subcultures do not exist and that we all '**drift**' between conformity and deviant '**subterranean values**'.
- **Marxists** argue that strain and subcultural theories ignore corporate crime. Marxist subcultural theorists such as Brake (1980) argue that working-class subcultures, such as punk and skinhead youth subcultures, develop as a resistance to capitalism rather than through strain.
- **Feminists** argue that strain and subcultural theories are 'malestream' and ignore female crime and deviancy, such as the increase in 'girl gangs'.
- **Postmodernists** such as Maffesoli (1996) argue that rather than there being rigid subcultures resulting from reasons such as strain, young people belong to 'neo-tribes' that are fluid and diverse. Rather than being based on deviant working-class values, neo-tribes result from different lifestyles that are influenced by a range of factors that are often media-led.

> **Knowledge check 1**
>
> Outline two criticisms of subcultural theories of crime.

Interactionism: labelling theory

Interactionists disagree with the functionalist view of crime and deviance in a number of ways:

- Rather than deviance producing social control, interactionists argue that agents of social control are the cause of crime and deviance.
- Rather than taking an absolute definition of deviance, interactionists adopt a relative definition and argue that there is no fixed view of what constitutes deviant behaviour.

Crime and deviance

- Rather than official statistics being reliable and generally accurately reflecting patterns of crime, interactionists regard them as being socially constructed and lacking validity. **Phenomenologist** Cicourel argues that due to police using typifications, crime statistics say more about the way the police operate than actual levels of crime.

Interactionists focus on **labelling theory** and how agents of social control such as the police, judiciary and the media have the power to define less powerful groups as deviant. **Becker** (1967) argues social groups create deviance by making rules and then labelling those who do not conform to these social controls as 'outsiders'. He argues that '**moral entrepreneurs**' have power over individuals and are able to redefine behaviour and laws into what they feel is acceptable.

Lemert (1951) differentiates between **primary deviance**, which constitutes deviant acts that have not been labelled, and **secondary** deviance, which is the **societal reaction** caused by acts being publicly labelled. For labelling theorists, societal reaction to being labelled as deviant has many different consequences:

- The individual can be **stigmatised** and excluded from 'normal society', as **Goffman** demonstrated when people are labelled as mentally ill.
- The label can become an individual's '**master status**' — the main way that others see them (e.g. being viewed as a 'junkie' rather than a father or boss). This is likely to have a negative impact on an individual's self-concept and a **self-fulfilling prophecy** will occur as they will begin to see their identity in terms of the label.
- **Becker** argues that further societal reaction, such as discrimination in the workplace, may lead to the labelled person following a '**deviant career**', resulting in them joining a subculture who have been similarly labelled.
- **Young's** (1971) study of hippy drug users illustrates how aspects of secondary deviancy such as police persecution and labelling led to a self-fulfilling prophecy where drug-taking and other subcultural deviant behaviour increased. This process, where labelling and an increased attempt to control behaviour actually create more deviance, is called the **deviancy amplification spiral**.
- **S. Cohen's** (1972) study of mods and rockers (see Table 5) is another example of how labelling, in this case by the media, can lead to deviant amplification via a **moral panic**.
- **Braithwaite** (1989) distinguishes between **disintegrative shaming**, where the criminal is negatively labelled and excluded from society, and **reintegrative shaming**, which labels the act as bad but not the person themselves. Braithwaite argues that reintegrative shaming avoids the negative effects of societal reaction and can lead to lower levels of crime as offenders will be made aware of the impact of their behaviour and will be accepted back into society without being stigmatised.

Typifications Shared concepts used to make sense of the world such as stereotypes that working-class or black people are more criminal than other groups.

Evaluation

- **+** Interactionism illustrates how deviance is a relative concept and how deviance, crime and crime statistics can be socially constructed.
- **+** It draws attention to the importance of labelling and its consequences.
- **+** It demonstrates the impact of agents of social control at a micro level and how they may create more deviance.
- **−** Labelling theory is too deterministic as individuals can reject labels and not follow the deviant career. However, Becker does acknowledge that individuals have the power to resist labels.
- **−** Labelling theory only focuses on trivial forms of deviance and is not useful in explaining more serious crimes, such as murder.
- **−** **Akers** (1967) criticises labelling theory for blaming societal reaction for an individual's deviant behaviour. He feels the act itself is more important than societal reaction and that individuals are aware that they are breaking the law.
- **−** Interactionism fails to explain why people commit deviant acts in the first place.
- **−** **Left realists** argue that labelling is too sympathetic to the criminal and ignores the victims of crime.
- **−** **Marxists** argue that it ignores the wider, macro origins of labelling and that labelling reflects the power of the ruling class in a capitalist society.

Knowledge check 2

Outline two strengths of interactionist theories of crime.

Marxism

Rather than social control benefiting everyone, as functionalists suggest, Marxists argue that it benefits the ruling class and works against working-class interests by preventing them rebelling against the injustices of capitalism. Marxists agree with interactionist criticisms of the functionalist view of crime and deviance that official statistics on crime are invalid due to the law being selectively enforced by powerful groups. However, traditional Marxists argue that this occurs at a macro rather than micro level. They argue that the structure of capitalist society can be seen to explain the causes of crime in three ways:

1 Capitalism is **criminogenic**. By its very exploitative nature, capitalism results in class inequality and poverty. **Gordon** (1976) suggests that higher levels of working-class crime are a response to this inequality. He argues that the emphasis on greed, profits, competition and materialism means that crime is a rational response by all social classes to capitalism. This is demonstrated in **white-collar crimes**, such as tax evasion and fiddling expenses, and **corporate crime**, such as health and safety violations, share-price fixing and environmental offences caused by pollution. Advertising is seen as encouraging crimes such as theft as a way to acquire the latest 'must-have' goods. Marxists further argue that increasing alienation (see under Marxism in the Theory and methods section) of the working class can cause non-utilitarian crime such as vandalism and violent behaviour.

2 **Selective law making and enforcement** Marxists argue that the law reflects ruling-class interest rather than the will of the people as functionalists suggest. **Snider** (1997) argues that laws that threaten the profit of big business, such as fair trade laws and health and safety legislation, are unlikely to be passed or enforced beyond a minimum level. **Chambliss** (1970) argues that laws to protect private

property are used by the ruling class to maintain the capitalist economy and keep the working class away from its spoils.

3 **Ideological** functions of crime and deviance. **Althusser** (1969) argues that the law is an **ideological state apparatus** which serves the interests of capitalists by maintaining and legitimating class inequality. Selective law enforcement, such as targeting social security 'scroungers', benefits the rich and powerful as tax fraudsters are rarely taken to court as their crimes are less likely to be treated as criminal offences. **Reiman** (2001) suggests that white-collar and corporate crimes are under-policed and under-punished. **Pearce** (1976) argues that the real purpose of laws seemingly passed in the interest of the working class, such as health and safety laws, is to serve capitalism by helping to ensure safe and loyal workers. The occasional prosecution will give the impression that the law is applied fairly and shows the 'caring side' of capitalism.

Marxists argue that crime statistics will reflect **selective law enforcement** and this, coupled with biased media coverage, will give the impression that crime is a working-class phenomenon. This will result in working-class people blaming working-class criminals for the problems they experience, such as low pay, which capitalism is causing. Conversely, **white-collar crime** and **corporate crime** are not seen as a serious problem by the public despite their being more costly to society. There are a number of reasons for this, such as the invisibility of the offences, the lack of a clear victim or knowledge of the offender. Corporate crime in particular is less likely to be prosecuted for a number of reasons — it is more complex; responsibility for it is often diffused and protected by powerful interests such as the state; it is dealt with internally to protect the company's reputation.

The New Criminology, I. Taylor et al. (1973), while agreeing with traditional Marxists on issues such as criminogenic capitalism and selective law enforcement, argues that a **fully social analysis** is required. This **neo-Marxist** approach combined the traditional Marxist views on inequality with the micro approach of labelling theory and its emphasis on societal reaction and individual meanings. The New Criminology is often referred to as **critical criminology** as it argues that the sociology of crime and deviance must be critical of the established capitalist order. It also takes on a more **voluntaristic** approach, arguing that individuals have free will and are able to commit crime for political reasons in response to injustices of the capitalist system. The New Criminology provides a framework for research based on seven micro and macro factors which it was felt needed to be adopted to produce a fully social theory. This approach was adopted by neo-Marxist Hall in his study on black muggers (see the Ethnicity and crime section).

Marxist subcultural theory, which was developed by the Centre for Contemporary Cultural Studies (CCCS), argued that the working-class youth subcultures developed their styles of clothes, music and language as a form of resistance to the inequality of capitalist society.

- **P. Cohen** (1972) described how 1970s skinheads reacted to the decline of working-class communities through symbols, exaggerating the clothes of the traditional manual worker, such as Dr Marten boots, and asserted their working-class masculinity through football violence.

Exam tip

Compare this view of selective law enforcement with labelling theory, which fails to locate it within a wider social context — i.e. how bias in the legal system benefits capitalism.

Exam tip

Be prepared to link points to general Marxist theory. The belief that the law acts in the interests of workers is an example of the false-consciousness that Marx argued existed among the working class.

Exam tip

The ideological nature of the law and its selective enforcement can be seen in Hall's book *Policing the Crisis*. In this moral panic the media scapegoated black muggers for the problems in capitalism at the time. Hall argued that this had the effect of dividing white against black working class, who were blamed for the problems in society, rather than capitalism.

- **Brake** (1980) argues that such resistance is 'magical' — an illusion that only appears to solve their problems. He argued that each generation of working-class youth subcultures have resisted their exploitative situation though different sorts of music, clothes etc.
- **Hebdige** (1979) outlined how punks 'resisted through rituals' by deliberately shocking the establishment through their use of deviant symbols, such Mohican haircuts, swastikas and bondage on clothing. However, he argued that the deviant styles that subcultures used would soon be commercialised by capitalism and available in high street retailers — such as punks' DIY ripped jeans with safety pins being quickly available in Topshop.

Evaluation

- + Marxist theory of crime demonstrates how the law reflects differences in power between social groups.
- + It highlights the impact of selective law enforcement and how corporate and white-collar crime is under-policed.
- + It has drawn attention to how inequality in society can lead to criminal behaviour.
- – Marxism is too deterministic and does not explain why not all working-class people who experience poverty commit crime.
- – **The New Criminology** accuses Marxism of being **economically deterministic**, arguing that not all crime is caused by economic factors.
- – The assumption that the end of capitalism will lead to the end of crime is rejected. Capitalism does not appear to be criminogenic in countries such as Japan or Singapore, which have a very low crime rate.
- – Traditional Marxist theory has been accused of ignoring the relationship between ethnicity and crime and deviance.
- – **Left realists** argue that, by focusing on the crimes of the powerful, Marxists neglect the fact that working-class people are the main victims of working-class crime.
- – **Right realists** agree and also argue that Marxism is too critical of the role of the police and the courts, which are a necessary part of social control.
- – **Functionalists** would argue that the law is applied equally and that there are numerous examples of the criminal justice system (CJS) acting against the interests of the ruling class, such as MPs' expenses.
- – **Feminists** argue that different types of Marxist theory ignore the patriarchal nature of the law and social control.
- – The New Criminology only provided a framework and did not conduct any research themselves. The 'fully social analysis' they advocated incorporates seven aspects of crime that were very complex.
- – The New Criminology has been criticised for its emphasis of the political nature of crimes, which is not useful for explaining crimes such as domestic violence and child abuse.
- – Marxist subcultural theory has been accused of underestimating the extent to which youth subcultures are influenced by the consumerism of capitalism and popular culture from the USA, such as 'gansta rap' and 'Nike identities'.

Knowledge check 3

Outline two criticisms made by left realists of Marxist theories of crime.

Realist approaches to the causes of crime and deviance

Table 3 Similarities and differences between right and left realists

Similarities	Differences	
Ideas	**Left realists**	**Right realists**
Crime is a real, growing problem that is damaging communities, particularly in urban areas	**Relative deprivation** Due to the media and consumerism, we are more aware of how deprived we are in relation to others. This may lead to crime as people feel resentment when they feel others 'unfairly' have more than them, e.g. steal the latest iPhone	**Biological differences** Wilson and Herrnstein (1985) claim some people are naturally more aggressive, extrovert and have low intelligence and so commit more crime due to biologically determined factors
Individualism and the pursuit of self-interest lead to the breakdown of family structure and the community and can lead to crime	**Marginalisation** Groups such as unemployed youth and ethnic minorities may feel powerless as they have no one to represent them. They may turn to crime such as vandalism or violence out of resentment or frustration	**Socialisation** Some families, particularly lone-parent, fail to teach correct values such as self-control often due to the lack of a male role model. Murray (1990) felt that there was a growing underclass who do not share the values of society and so are more likely to commit crime
Realists agree that labelling and different Marxist theories are too sympathetic towards the working-class criminal	**Subculture** As a consequence of relative deprivation and marginalisation, some working-class and black people may seek a collective response and form deviant subcultures. Due to their blocked opportunities, some may turn to street crime	**Rational choice** Clarke (1980) argued that individuals rationally choose to commit crime because the costs are outweighed by the benefits. Felson (1998) argued that if a motivated offender was in the presence of a 'capable guardian' they would act rationally and not offend

Exam tip

Relate the right realism to the New Right views of Murray on the importance of the nuclear family and it being undermined by the welfare state, creating a dependency culture. It is argued that social policies on reducing dependency on welfare, such as cutting benefits, can also help reduce crime by encouraging individuals to be more self-reliant. By working, people will be financially independent and will be less likely to be involved in street crime.

Evaluation

+ Left realists have drawn attention towards the reality and fear of crime that exists for some deprived groups.
+ Both realist theories have been influential in social policies aimed at tackling crime (see the section on realist approaches to crime prevention).
− **Hughes** (1991) argues that left realists fail to explain why some people who are relatively deprived commit crime and others do not.
− By focusing on property crime and inner-city crime, left realists fail to provide evidence to support a representative theory of crime.
− Left realists' use of subcultural theory and the assumption that crime occurs when there is no value consensus has been criticised. **Marxists** would argue

Exam tip

While right realists generally argue that poor values cannot be changed, Wilson and Herrnstein (1985) argue that individuals with a biological predisposition to commit crime can be 'trained away' from it with the right socialisation. However, the underlying causes of crime are very difficult to change.

that left realism has strayed too far away from Marxist views in adopting functionalist concepts to explain crime.

- **Lilly et al.** (2002) reject the biological argument of right realists. They found that only 3% of differences in offending could be explained by differences in intelligence levels.
- While rational choice may be useful to explain some utilitarian crime, it cannot explain violent crime and crimes committed under the influence of alcohol or drugs.
- There is a contradiction between criminals making rational choices and having low intelligence and being poorly socialised.
- **Marxists** and **left realists** argue that right realists ignore wider structural causes of crime such as poverty and social exclusion.
- **Marxists** argue that both realist theories neglect corporate crime, which is more damaging to society.

■ The social construction of crime statistics

- Police crime statistics have been collected since 1857 and are now published quarterly by the government. The statistics are useful in showing patterns and trends in offending. However, there are a number of reasons why official crime statistics (OCS) may not show the real rate of crime:
  1 Crime may not be reported to the police for a number of reasons, such as fear of reprisals, distrust or lack of faith in the police, the trivial nature of the crime, and embarrassment.
  2 The police do not record all crimes due to reasons such as a lack of evidence, offences seen as too trivial and the negative impact on their clear-up rates, and chances of promotion.
- Another way of estimating patterns of offending are **victimisation** (or victim) **surveys**, in which individuals are asked for details about crime committed against them, typically in the last year. The **British Crime Survey (BCS)**, now called the **Crime Survey of England and Wales (CSEW)**, has been conducted by the government since 1981 and includes a large sample (now around 50,000 people).
- Both OCS and the BCS have revealed that crime increased rapidly between the mid-1980s to 1993 but has decreased since then. Figures from the CSEW in 2015 saw a 7% decrease in crime compared to the previous year, and the lowest estimate since the BCS began in 1981. The findings of BCS/CSEW suggest that only a quarter of crimes are reported to the police, illustrating that police-recorded crimes may be only the tip of the iceberg in the case of some crimes.
- The BCS/CSEW and other victimisation surveys have revealed that the 'fear of crime', is increasing, particularly for those living in socially deprived areas. Despite the evidence to the contrary, two thirds of the respondents to the BCS/CSEW consistently state that they believe crime has increased a little or a lot over the last decade.

Exam tip

For a question on the views of realist theories on the causes of crime, be prepared to refer to their different crime prevention strategies (see the section on realist approaches to crime prevention).

Knowledge check 4

Outline two areas of agreement between left and right realists.

- Lea and Young used their own victimisation survey, the Islington Crime Survey (1986), to illustrate their 'realist' approach and to demonstrate that the fear of crime was a genuine fear among the working class and other marginalised groups living in deprived areas. Unlike other Marxist-influenced approaches to crime, they argue that official statistics do reflect real patterns of crime.

- Despite the BCS/CSEW being more valid than OCS, as it includes crimes not reported to the police and so shows the **'dark figure of crime'**, it has a number of drawbacks:

  1 It does not survey all crimes, e.g. theft committed against businesses, corporate crime and victimless crimes such as prostitution.

  2 It only recently included those under 16 years of age.

  3 People may not be aware that they are a victim of crime, e.g. children or in crimes such as fraud.

  4 Victims' memories of crime may be inaccurate, e.g. due to the trauma experienced.

  5 Despite the survey being anonymous, people may not admit to being victims of crimes such as sexual offences.

- **Self-report studies** ask respondents to reveal crimes they have committed and provide another useful alternative to OCS. For example, they reveal that middle-class males are just as likely to offend as working-class males. However, these studies may lack validity due to respondents believing that their crimes might be reported to the police.

- OCS suggest that crime is largely a working-class phenomenon. The vast majority of the prison population are from socially deprived backgrounds and most people who appear in court are from working-class backgrounds. As has been outlined in the previous section, different sociological theories have different explanations regarding why members of the working class appear disproportionally in official crime statistics. While those who adopt a positivist approach, such as functionalists, accept the validity of OCS to show a realistic picture of crime, theories based on an interpretivist approach argue that OCS are **socially constructed** and are based on the institutional biases of the criminal justice system. Marxists would agree that the law is selectively enforced and would argue that offences associated with the middle class, such as white-collar crimes, are largely ignored, whereas working-class offences, such as street crime, are targeted by the police.

Exam tip

For an essay involving theoretical explanations of crime for both class and ethnicity, be prepared to refer to the methodological approach adopted by left realists Lea and Young.

Dark figure of crime
The unknown amount of crime that is never revealed. This applies more to crimes that are less visible, such as white-collar crime, and crimes of a sexual nature such as rape.

Knowledge check 5

Outline two strengths of victimisation studies.

Summary

After studying this section, you should be aware of sociological explanations of crime, deviance, social order and social control. You should be familiar with the following:
- functionalism, strain and subcultural explanations
- Marxism and neo-Marxist explanations
- labelling theory and the social construction of crime
- right and left realist approaches to the causes of crime and deviance
- sociological explanations of patterns of crime in relation to social class, e.g. selective law enforcement and white-collar crime
- different methods of measuring crime: official crime statistics, and victimisation and self-report surveys

■ Ethnicity and crime

- Black people, and to a lesser extent Asians, are over-represented in OCS at all stages of the criminal justice system (CJS). In 2014, 10% of the British prison population were black and 6% were Asian. For black people this was significantly higher than the 2.8% of the general population they represented (Asians made up 6% of the population). Interpretivists argue that such statistics reflect levels of discrimination towards ethnic minorities (EMs) rather than real rates of offending and have made several criticisms of the CJS.

- **Phillips and Browning** (2007) argue that EM communities are likely to feel 'over-policed and under protected'. This is reflected in statistics from 2011 showing that black people are seven times as likely (Asians twice as likely) as white people to be **stopped and searched** by the police. Phillips and Browning suggest that as a result of this deliberate targeting by the police, some black people act out the label of potential criminal and commit street crime.

- **Holdaway** (1983) observed a **canteen culture** in the police that was racist and influenced officers' decisions to stop and search black people. Following the inquest into the death of the young black teenager Stephen Lawrence, the **Macpherson Report** (1999) concluded that there was **institutional racism** in the Metropolitan Police.

- However, the **demographic explanation** argues that statistics may just reflect the fact that EMs are over-represented in population groups most likely to be stopped and searched, such as young people in inner-city areas. Waddington et al. (2004) found this to be the factor that shaped stop and search policies of the police rather than any racial discrimination.

- There is also evidence of racism in the **judicial process**. Hood (1992) found that black males were more likely than white males to receive custodial sentences for the same offences. While Asians and black people are less likely to be found guilty than whites, this may be due to police stereotyping bringing cases to court against EMs with weaker evidence.

- Victim surveys also tend to suggest higher rates of offending by black people. They also show a high level of intra-ethnic crime, i.e. crime that takes place within ethnic groups. Self-report studies, however, do not support the view that black people are more likely to offend than whites and also show that Asians are less likely to offend.

Table 4 applies theories of crime and deviance to the issue of ethnicity and includes the two main explanations for ethnic differences in crime statistics, neo-Marxist and left realist. For more detail and evaluation of these theories, refer back to the section on sociological theories of crime and deviance.

> **Canteen culture** A term used by Holdaway to describe the occupational culture that existed in the police force that was characterised by racist (and sexist) attitudes.

> ### Exam tip
> Be prepared to link moral panics to a discussion on the social construction of OCS in relation to ethnic minorities. In addition to Hall's moral panic, refer also to how the post 9/11 moral panic of Islamophobia may have contributed to the police targeting Asians. For example, Asians are three times more likely to be stopped and searched under the 2000 Terrorism Act than any other group.

Table 4 Sociological explanations of ethnicity and crime

Theory	Explanation	Key concepts / studies
Functionalist	Lack of goals or institutional means. EM groups innovate due to the racism they experience	Merton — EMs experience **anomie**
Right realist (New Right)	Due to poor **socialisation** and being in a lone-parent family, some EMs are more likely to be part of an underclass and live a life of crime	Murray (1990) Underclass Dependency culture
Interactionist	EMs are more likely to be negatively **labelled** by agents of social control, and therefore appear disproportionately on crime statistics	Phillips and Bowling (2007) Labelling and self-fulfilling prophecy
Marxist	EMs are more likely to be working class and commit crime targeted by agents of social control	**Selective law enforcement**
Neo-Marxist	1 *Policing the Crisis* — The police released statistics suggesting that black Britons were more likely to be involved in street crime. Black youth was a **scapegoat** used to divert attention away from the problems of capitalism. This led to more aggressive policing, e.g. stop and search policy 2 Gilroy — *The myth of black criminality*. Police target young black Britons. Their crime is **politically motivated** and is a reaction to racism	1 Hall (1978) Moral panic (black muggers). Black youth portrayed as a folk devil via **media labelling** 2 Gilroy (1982) **Police labelling** Institutional racism
Left realist	OCS reflect real differences in EM offending. Structural opportunities for EMs are blocked by racism, which leads to **social exclusion**. As a result EMs are more likely to feel poor and turn to crime, often with other like-minded people, e.g. in street gangs	Lea and Young (1993) — EM crime is caused by: ■ marginalisation ■ relative deprivation ■ criminal subculture

Evaluation

- Left realists reject interactionist and neo-Marxist views that OCS are socially constructed and instead argue that they reflect real fears, e.g. about mugging. They argue that while police racism exists it cannot on its own explain ethnic patterns of crime, such as why conviction rates for Asians are lower than those for black people.
- Hall has been criticised for assuming the white working class were 'panicking' and blaming crime on black people and for not explaining how the moral panic was created.
- Gilroy's view of black crime as being political has been criticised for failing to acknowledge that most black crime is committed against other black people and therefore cannot be politically motivated.
- Left realists have been criticised for underestimating the impact of police racism. For example, there has been an increase in the Muslim prison population from 7.7% in 2002 to 14.4% in 2015, which conflict theorists would argue is linked to Muslims being viewed as the new 'enemy within' by the authorities since 9/11.

Knowledge check 6

Outline two ways in which it has been argued that the CJS is racist.

■ Gender and crime

Female crime

- According to the Prison Reform Trust, women made up only 4.5% of the prison population in October 2015. Four out of every five recorded crimes are committed by males and there are significant gender differences in offending. Males are much more likely to be convicted of violent or sexual offences, whereas 81% of women entered prison for non-violent offences. In comparison, theft and handling offences were the two highest offences for which women received custodial sentences.

- One explanation as to why women appear less in the OCS is the **chivalry thesis** developed by **Pollock** (1950), which argues that the CJS is more lenient towards women. This is due to males being socialised into being protective towards females.

- Evidence from self-report studies supports the view that women are treated more leniently. **Campbell** (1981) and **Graham and Bowling** (1993) both discovered that females committed a lot more crime than the OCS suggested. Campbell also found that women are more likely than males to be cautioned for committing the same offence.

- However, evidence from **Box's** (1981) self-report study suggests that women who commit serious offences are not treated more leniently than males. Farrington and Morris (1983) found that this was also the case in magistrates' courts.

- In terms of sexual offences, evidence suggests that the CJS is biased **against** women. **Casborn** (1985) and **Heidensohn** (1996) found that courts are more severe on female juveniles when it comes to crimes related to sexual promiscuity. **Walklate** (2001) argues that in rape cases it is often the female victim rather than the male offender who is on trial.

- Whether chivalry in the CJS exists is open to debate but what is clear is that women have a lower offending rate than males. A number of explanations have been put forward to explain this:

  1 **Functionalist sex role theory** Parsons (1955) argues that differences in crime and deviance are due to **differential socialisation** in the family, such as girls being brought up to fulfil the expressive role and boys being encouraged to be tough and take risks. While early feminist explanations such as those of **Smart** (1977) accept the significance of differential socialisation, they argue that it reflects patriarchy and needs to be changed. Feminists are also critical of functionalists for basing their ideas on biological assumptions about females being more naturally responsible for caring for others.

  2 **Patriarchal control** Heidensohn (1985) argues that women have fewer opportunities to commit crime due to their being socially controlled by patriarchy in three ways:

     - **In the home** Due to their role as housewife and mother, women have less opportunity for crime. Daughters are also more closely controlled in the family, such as being given less freedom to go out at night.

Knowledge check 7

Outline two criticisms of the chivalry thesis.

Exam tip

Be prepared to apply other functionalist-based arguments to a discussion of gender and crime. Subcultural theorists such as Cohen and Miller argue that the culture and values of working-class boys lead to crime and deviance. Also New Right thinker Murray argues that the lack of a male role model in single-parent families can encourage males to take up criminal behaviour.

- **In public** Women are less likely to go into public places where deviance occurs, particularly at night due to a fear of violence such as sexual attacks. Women's behaviour is also controlled through the fear of acquiring a bad reputation, such as being labelled as a 'slag' or 'bitch'.
- **In the workplace** Women's lack of opportunities in the workplace, illustrated by the gender pay gap and the glass ceiling, mean that women will have fewer opportunities for crime, particularly white-collar crime. Heidensohn quotes research which found that as many as 60% of women have suffered some form of sexual harassment at work, showing this to be another form of patriarchal control experienced by many women.

3 **Class and gender 'deals'** Drawing on **Hirschi's** (1969) control theory (see the section on realist approaches to crime prevention), **Carlen** (1988) argues that working-class women commit crime only when they lack the controls that prevent most people from committing crime. The two main controls are the **class deal** (financial security) and the **gender deal** (emotional attachment to family life). In a study of 39 women who had been convicted of crime, 32 had always been in poverty (lacked the class deal) and most had either been in care or had experienced some form of sexual violence (lacking the gender deal). Carlen concluded that for these women, crime was a rational response to the lack of class and/or gender deals and was the only route to a decent living. Both Heidensohn and Carlen combine feminist and control theories to explain why females commit less crime. However, as Heidensohn acknowledges, control theory can be criticised for portraying women as passive victims.

4 **Liberation theory Adler** (1975) argues that increasing rates of female crime can be explained by women's liberation. As society becomes less patriarchal, women will have greater confidence and opportunities to commit the same crimes as men. Denscombe (2001) suggests that young females are engaging in more risk-taking behaviour and are adopting more traditionally male attitudes such as 'looking hard'.

5 **The feminisation of poverty** Rather than liberation, some feminists point to the increased marginalisation of women since the 1980s as they have become more likely than men to experience poverty due to low pay and benefit reductions. Heidensohn (2002) argues that most female criminals are working class and commit crimes such as shoplifting and prostitution out of economic necessity rather than liberation.

Masculinity and crime

- **Messerschmidt** (1993) argues that crime and deviance are one way that men can accomplish masculinity. The dominant form of masculinity that boys are socialised into is **hegemonic masculinity**, which stresses differences from women and is defined by goals such as: being a breadwinner; having power over others, particularly females; treating females as sexual objects; toughness and risk-taking behaviour. Some men not may not want (e.g. gay men) or may be unable to achieve these goals and may turn to crime to accomplish different (or subordinated) masculinities. For example, white working-class males who may underachieve may develop anti-school cultures based on toughness or non-conformity to achieve a

Exam tip

Be prepared to evaluate more 'dated' explanations with contemporary evidence. As a result of this type of control, McRobbie (1978) argues that girls developed a bedroom culture which restricted their opportunities for crime. Since then there has not only been an increase in girl gangs but the advent of online gaming has arguably led to a bedroom culture for boys who may be socialising with friends at home or online rather than 'on the street'.

Exam tip

While sociologists tend to reject biological factors, they cannot be ignored and could be discussed briefly in an essay on gender and crime. For example, premenstrual tension has been accepted as a form of defence in courts since the 1980s.

subordinated masculinity in school, whereas black working-class boys may turn to violent street gangs outside of school.

- Messerschmidt notes that middle-class men may also be motivated by a masculine value system but will turn to white-collar or corporate crime to accomplish hegemonic masculinity.
- Messerschmidt has been criticised for not explaining why only a minority of men turn to crime to accomplish their hegemonic masculinity goals. It is also argued that masculinity may be just one way that crime is expressed, e.g. toughness, rather than being a cause of crime.
- In the late (or post) modern era **deindustrialisation** has meant that some working-class men can no longer achieve their masculinity through traditional forms of employment. **Winlow's** (2001) study of bouncers in Sunderland illustrates how the 'night-time economy' has provided opportunities to demonstrate their masculinity through violence as well as additional 'perks' to their paid work in the form of money gained through illegal activities such as drug dealing.

Deindustrialisation
The process whereby the traditional manufacturing sector in countries like the UK has declined, due to the growth of the global economy. This has resulted in the reduction of manual jobs, leading to unemployment, poverty and crime.

Summary

After studying these sections, you should be aware of the social distribution of crime and deviance by ethnicity, gender and social class, including recent patterns and trends in crime. You should be familiar with the following:
- patterns of crime in relation to gender and ethnicity
- sociological explanations of patterns of crime in relation to ethnicity e.g. racism and the criminal justice system
- sociological explanations of patterns of crime in relation to females, e.g. the chivalry thesis, sex role theory and feminism
- sociological explanations of patterns of crime in relation to males, e.g. masculinity and crime

■ Globalisation and crime

- Globalisation, the increasing interconnectedness of societies, has been spread by a number of factors such as the growth of global media, global markets, mass migration and tourism. **Held et al.** (1999) suggest that globalisation has led to the spread of transnational organised crime, creating new opportunities for existing crime but also creating new ways of committing crime. For example, greater communication and travel have enabled the drugs industry to transcend national boundaries. Other examples include human and arms trafficking, cybercrime, green crime and international terrorism.
- In 1988 **Castells** suggested that the global criminal economy was worth over £1 trillion per year. The illegal drugs trade illustrates how global criminal networks have developed to meet the demands of the West. The supply of drugs is met by farmers in countries such as Colombia, who will make more money growing illegal crops than conventional crops to meet this demand. As a result, cocaine production outsells all of Colombia's other exports combined.
- **Hobbs** (1998) argues that crime is no longer just local but **'glocal'**, as it involves networks of people across the globe. Rather than being based on old mafia-style fixed hierarchies, criminal networks are increasingly more fluid. As well as drugs,

other examples of glocal trade are trafficking women and children for prostitution and slavery, and smuggling legal and stolen goods to sell on foreign markets.

- **Gleeny** (2008) traces the spread of modern transnational crime to the break-up of the Soviet Union and Eastern Bloc and the simultaneous deregulation of global markets. In Russia this created opportunities for a new capitalist class (often ex-Communist officials) to make vast sums of money selling the country's natural resources, such as gas, on global markets. To protect their wealth these 'oligarchs' turned to new '**McMafias**', comprised of ex-Communist secret service employees, police etc. and former criminals. Again, these criminal networks were not organised like the traditional Mafia, and groups such as the Chechens would even 'franchise' their business to other parts of the globe.
- From a Marxist perspective, **Taylor** (1997) looks at the impact of transnational corporations (TNCs) on global crime. Globalisation has allowed TNCs to more easily switch production to developing countries. This not only exploits workers in low-wage countries but creates unemployment and poverty, leading to an increase in domestic crime. Deregulation and the fact that global crime is difficult to police has meant it has been easier for elite groups and TNCs to commit crimes such as tax evasion.
- **Beck** (1992) argues that the new insecurities of the late-modern era have led to a **global risk consciousness**, such as the threat of migration or global terrorism. The public demand to deal with such risks, often fuelled by sensationalist media coverage, has led to Western governments increasing methods of social control, such as tighter border controls and the use of surveillance technology (see the Liquid surveillance section).

■ Green crime

- Green crimes are crimes against the environment. These crimes can have a negative impact on both humanity and the environment.
- Due to **globalisation** and the fact that the planet is a single ecosystem, green crime is on the increase. Environmental disasters, such as the nuclear accident in Chernobyl and the BP oil spillage in the Gulf of Mexico, are not restricted to nation-state boundaries.
- **Conflict theorists** such as Marxists would argue that green crime is largely committed by powerful groups such as BP and other TNCs that work hand in hand with powerful elites, e.g. politicians in government.
- **Late-modern** theorist **Beck** argues that we are living in a '**global-risk society**' that has been brought about by the need for the increased demands for consumer goods. The resultant increase in production has led to 'manufactured risks', such as the increase in greenhouse gas emissions which contribute to global warming.
- **Green criminology** transgresses (oversteps) the boundaries of **traditional criminology**, which only studies patterns and causes of law-breaking. **White** (2008) argues that current laws are inadequate and that green crime should be defined as any crime that causes harm even if it is not illegal. He argues that green crimes such as deforestation of the rainforests are not being adequately dealt with by internal law, due to the influence of TNCs such McDonalds.

Knowledge check 8

Outline two ways in which the 'McMafias' differ from the Mafia.

Exam tip

Be prepared to relate the impact of globalisation on domestic crime to Lea and Young's left realist explanation of the causes of crime. Increased job insecurity resulting from globalisation and deindustrialisation will lead to a lack of legitimate opportunity structures required to achieve the material goals of society. This, alongside advertising of global consumer products that the socially excluded cannot afford, is likely to increase feelings of relative deprivation, which may lead to crime.

- White also argues that green criminology takes an **ecocentric** view, which sees environmental harm as being interconnected with the future of human well-being. This contrasts with the **anthropocentric** view favoured by TNCs that humans have a right to exploit the resources of the planet, including animals, for their own benefit.
- **South** (2008) suggests that there are two types of green crime:
  1 **Primary** green crimes are the direct result of the destruction and degradation of the Earth's resources, e.g. air pollution, deforestation, abusing animal rights and water pollution.
  2 **Secondary** green crimes involve the flouting of existing laws and regulations, e.g. dumping toxic waste and breaching health and safety rules, such as in the cases of Bhopal and Chernobyl.

Evaluation of green crime

+ Green crime draws attention to the increase in manufactured global risks and global environmental concerns.
+ It identifies the need to address the impact of environmental damage to both humans and the other species on the planet.
− Green crime's emphasis on harm means that it is based on subjective opinions. There are no clear boundaries in terms of defining or studying green crime.

> **Knowledge check 9**
>
> What is the difference between traditional and green criminology?

■ Human rights and state crimes

- State crimes are illegal activities that break national or international laws and which are carried out by or on behalf of governments. **McLaughlin** (2001) outlines four types of state crime:
  1 Political crimes, e.g. corruption and censorship of the media, carried out by politicians and civil servants
  2 Crimes by the police, armed services and secret services, e.g. deaths in police custody, torture and ethnic cleansing
  3 Economic crime, e.g. official violations of health and safety laws
  4 Social and cultural crimes, e.g. institutional racism
- **Schwendinger** (1970) argues that crime should be viewed as a violation of people's basic human rights, not just the breaking of laws, and that definitions of state crime should include human rights crimes. He suggests that states are guilty of committing crimes if they deny people equal opportunities by practising imperialism, racism, sexism, homophobia and economic exploitation.
- However, critics argue that Schwendinger's definition of human rights is too broad as he suggests that any violation of human rights should be defined as illegal. **S. Cohen** (1996; 2001) is critical of Schwendinger's view that state crime should include violations of human rights. He argues that there is no clear agreement that practices such as economic exploitation are criminal. There is also limited agreement on what counts as human rights. Cohen also argues that, due to the

power of governments and their ability to conceal and legitimate their crimes, the extent of state control is difficult to measure and, as a result, such crime is more 'invisible' than conventional crime.

- Cohen applies Sykes and Matza's **techniques of neutralisation** (see the Functionalism, strain and subcultural theories section) to examine how the state justifies its crimes against human rights. For example, the Nazi concentration camp guards would use 'denial of responsibility' by claiming that they were simply obeying orders. Government secret services may 'appeal to higher loyalties' by imprisoning people without trial in the name of national security.
- Critical criminologists such as Marxists would argue that powerful groups within the state are able to define their activities as legal. For example, as well as having the power to cover up their crimes though issuing legal restrictions on the media, governments are able to define what counts as a war crime. The use of military torture and the invasion of countries such as Iraq can be portrayed by UK and US governments as a necessary part of the 'war on terror'.
- Critics of this view would argue that so-called state crimes are not in fact criminal. They would reject the notion of 'state crime' and would argue that acts such as increased censorship and the curtailing of the human rights of suspected terrorists are necessary if committed in the national interest.

The media and crime

Media representations of crime

- Interactionists argue that rather than being objective and impartial, the news is socially constructed and is dependent to large extent on the **news values** of journalists and other media personnel. A key news value that helps to explain why crime and deviance make up such a large and disproportionate amount of news coverage is 'negativity': bad news is good news.
- However, as **Felson** (1998) states, media reporting of crime is distorted and he argues that it reinforces a number of fallacies or falsehoods about crime. These include: all age groups are involved in crime, the middle class are more likely to be victims of crime, the police are more efficient than they seem and that criminals are ingenious rather than opportunistic. Felson argues that the dramatic fallacy exaggerates violent and extraordinary crimes, promoting a fear of crime, particularly among vulnerable groups such as the elderly and women. Such fallacies are reinforced by fictional representations of crime in TV programmes, e.g the emphasis on violent and sexual crimes in crime dramas.

> **Exam tip**
>
> Be prepared to relate the left realist arguments to a question on the relationship between the media and crime. As well as media representations contributing to a 'fear of crime', Lea and Young point to the role the media play in causing relative deprivation. For example, the advertising of 'must-have' consumer goods further marginalises socially excluded groups, who may then be more likely to turn to crime.

> **Knowledge check 10**
>
> Outline two criticisms of Schwendinger's view that definitions of state crime should be extended to include human rights crimes.

> **Exam tip**
>
> Be prepared to link the topic of green crime to a question on state crime. Marxists would argue that state and green crimes often both involve crimes of the powerful. For example, nation-states can use their power to make laws in their own interest about what constitutes environmental harm.

News values The guidelines used by journalists and other media personnel to determine whether a story is newsworthy, i.e. interesting enough to attract readership or audience.

The media as a possible cause of crime

■ There has been much debate as to whether media content can have a negative effect on the behaviour of the audience, particularly vulnerable groups such as children. The **hypodermic syringe model (HSM)** argues that there is a direct correlation between real life violence and antisocial behaviour and that portrayed in film, song lyrics and computer games such as *Grand Theft Auto*.

■ **Newson** (1994) argues that long exposure to violence over the course of young people's lives has led to them becoming desensitised to violence, i.e. they have become socialised into accepting violent behaviour as normal. However, **Buckingham** (1993) claims that children are media literate and are able to differentiate between fictional violence in computer games such as *Call of Duty* and real-life violence. **Cumberbatch** (2004) reviewed over 3,500 research studies and felt that the evidence on the impact of media violence was inconclusive.

■ In addition to imitation of violence, the media have been seen to influence crime and deviance in a number of other ways, such as glamorising crime and providing information on how to commit crime. **Jewkes** (2003) also draws attention to how new types of media such as the internet have led to new opportunities for crime, particularly cybercrime such as email scams, data theft and illegal pornography. Jewkes also points to how new technology has given governments greater powers of surveillance such as CCTV cameras and digital fingerprinting (see the Liquid surveillance section).

Moral panics (MPs)

Interactionists argue that media labelling can cause crime through what **S. Cohen** (1972) described as a moral panic (MP). Cohen argues that MPs can lead to **deviancy amplification**, as occurred in his study of Mods and Rockers following the Easter Bank Holiday of 1964 — see Table 5.

Table 5 The stages of a MP as illustrated by Cohen's study *Folk Devils and Moral Panics*.

Stage	Cohen's mods and rockers
1 Media report on an event in an exaggerated way	Newspaper headline: 'Youngsters beat up town'
2 Reporting demonises the group as folk devils using **symbolisation**	Violent young rockers in leather jackets. Mods on customised scooters
3 Moral entrepreneurs react to the media reports	Politicians call for a crackdown on young thugs
4 The media predict further trouble	More violence at the next Bank Holiday
5 The authorities stamp down hard on the group	Greater police presence and more arrests
6 The group reacts to this response	Gangs become more deviant due to over-policing
7 The self-fulfilling prophecy and the **deviance amplification spiral** are complete	More arrests made and two distinctive youth subcultures formed

Crime and deviance

There are a number of sociological explanations for the formation of moral panics.

- Cohen argued that MPs occur at a time of 'moral crisis' when society is undergoing major social change. The media portrayed members of the new 'immoral' youth subcultures as folk devils, as they were viewed as challenging the traditional authority that they felt 'decent' people should subscribe to.
- **Functionalists** view MPs as a way in which society responds to **anomie** brought about by rapid social change. By focusing people's attention and moral outrage at the behaviour of the folk devil, the media can help uphold social solidarity and ensure that the public demand action to re-establish the status quo.
- **Neo-Marxist Hall** (1978) argues that MPs have ideological functions. He argues that the MP over black muggers divided the white working class against the black working class and, as a result, diverted attention away from the problems that were being faced by capitalism at the time.
- **Left realists** reject the view that MPs are simply the result of ruling-class ideology or the result of the biased news values of journalists. They argue that MPs reflect real concerns of marginalised groups, such as those living in inner-city areas.
- An alternative view is that journalists create MPs to sell more newspapers when there is a lack of news stories available.
- The strength of MPs from an interactionist perspective is that they have identified the role of the media in the social construction of crime and deviance.
- **McRobbie and Thornton** (1995) are also critical of MPs and argue that they are outdated. With the advent of new technology, such as 24-hour rolling news, they are becoming harder to sustain. It is argued that in the late-modern (or postmodern) era, MPs have less impact as the audience is now more active and able to challenge and reject media presentations of the news.

Exam tip

Be prepared to make the connection between moral panics and interactionist theory. You should understand and be able to apply concepts used in the description of MPs such as labelling, self-fulfilling prophecy, moral entrepreneurs and deviancy amplification.

Knowledge check 11

Outline two criticisms of the idea of moral panics.

Summary

After studying these sections, you should be aware of globalisation and crime in contemporary society; the media and crime; green crime; human rights and state crimes. You should be familiar with the following:

- how globalisation has created new opportunities for and ways of committing crime, e.g. transnational organised crime, global criminal organisations and crimes of the powerful

- different types of green crime and green criminology
- human rights and sociological explanations of state crime
- media representations of crime, the media as a cause of crime and moral panics

■ Crime control, punishment and victims

Realist approaches to crime prevention

Both right and left realists see crime as a real and increasing problem. While both feel that governments need to adopt practical strategies to reduce crime, they have very different solutions.

Table 6 Realist solutions to crime

Similarities	Differences	
	Left realists	**Right realists**
Need to get tough on crime	Need to get tough on the causes of crime	Crime cannot be solved, just controlled
The fear of crime is a rational response. Official statistics are reliable and show real patterns of crime and victimisation	**Social and community crime prevention (SCCP)** Policies need to tackle the root causes of crime, such as poverty and social exclusion	**Situational crime prevention (SCP) Target hardening** to deal with the 'rational choice' to offend by reducing opportunities for crime, e.g. security guards, CCTV, gated communities
Wilson and Kelling and left realists agree that a lack of community and informal controls can lead to crime	**Community-based policing** The police must build better relationships with and be more accountable to the local community (e.g. police community support officers, or PCSOs, should work with local schools)	**Environmental crime prevention (ECP)** Wilson and Kelling (1982). 'Broken windows' must be replaced immediately. Zero tolerance policing on minor crimes will also help stop neighbourhood decline
Marxists would argue they both focus on street crime and ignore corporate crime	**Selective law enforcement** does exist, e.g. institutional racism occurs and policing needs to be improved	The police are professional and impartial and are an important part of the practical solution to reduce crime

Specific policies

SCP

The Port Authority Bus Terminal in New York was reshaped to 'design out' crime, e.g. smaller sinks reduced the likelihood of the homeless using them to bathe.

Stoke Council introduced an improved street lighting scheme in one area, which reduced opportunities to commit street crime (crime was reduced by 26%).

ECP

In New York a **zero tolerance** policy of aggressive policing was adopted on minor crimes such as begging and fare dodging, and the Clean Car Program meant subway carriages with graffiti were immediately removed. The police proactively dealt with minor forms of disorder with the aim of preventing more serious crime.

SCCP

Sure Start aimed at tackling aspects of social exclusion by improving the educational opportunities of disadvantaged groups, such as the working class and ethnic minorities, and providing support for entering the labour market (such as preschool education and parenting classes).

> **Exam tip**
>
> You should link the 'broken windows' thesis of Wilson and Kelling to Hirshi's (1969) version of control theory, which argues that social bonds such as attachment hold society together and prevent people from committing crime. If minor crimes go unpunished, people will feel there is no social control in their community and start to feel detached from society, leading to crime.

The **Perry Pre-school** project in the USA gave an intellectual enrichment programme to a selected group of disadvantaged black 3–4-year-olds for 2 years. By the age of 40, those who had followed the programme had lower rates of crime and were more likely to be in employment than their peers.

Knowledge check 12

Outline two criticisms of SCP.

Evaluation

- While there is evidence that it can reduce certain types of crime by increasing the risks and effort to commit crime, a major criticism of SCP is **displacement**. Crime is not reduced, as criminals will rationally respond to target hardening by moving to where targets are softer. **Chaiken** et al. (1974) found that in New York a crackdown on subway robberies simply displaced them to the streets above.
+ Evidence also suggests that ECPs are effective. For example, in New York between 1993 and 1996 zero tolerance policies arguably led to a dramatic decline in most crimes (homicide rates fell by 50%).
- However, other reasons have been suggested for this reduction, such as a fall in unemployment, crack cocaine being less available, the NYPD (City of New York Police Department) employing 7,000 extra officers.
- The zero tolerance policy of 'three strikes and you're out' has led to a dramatic increase in the prison population in the USA. High rates of recidivism (repeat offending) would suggest that tougher sentencing and prison does not act as a deterrent and is not an effective policy of crime prevention.
- SCCP policies are often long-term solutions and it is difficult to measure their specific impact on crime reduction.
- Critics of left realist polices, such as right realists, argue that they are 'too soft' on criminals. They argue that individuals make rational choices to commit crimes and that crime is not caused by society.

Punishment and the role of prisons and surveillance

- Punishment, especially prison, is thought to reduce crime in the following ways:
  1 **Deterrence** Right realists argue that prison will increase the cost as against the benefit of crime, therefore deterring the criminal from making the rational choice to commit a crime.
  2 **Incapacitation** Right realists argue that prison is important as it removes the criminals from society so they cannot offend again.
  3 **Rehabilitation** Others see punishment such as prison as an opportunity to reform criminals through education and training so that they do not return to crime in the future.
- Functionalists such as **Durkheim** (1893) see the CJS as acting in the interests of society as a whole. He argues that public punishment of crimes is good for society as it leads to social solidarity and consensus as people would come together to condemn the criminal. Durkheim felt that in traditional societies punishment tended to be based on **retributive justice**, which tends to be severe and based

Exam tip

Be prepared to apply general evaluation points on the right realist and left realist theories of crime that these crime prevention strategies are based on (see the section on realist approaches to crime). For example, the criticism of the rational choice argument being useless to explain crimes such as being drunk and disorderly would suggest that even SCP strategies such as CCTV would do little to prevent this crime.

on revenge: 'an eye for an eye'. However, in a modern society punishment is more likely to be based on **restitutive justice** — to try to restore the situation, such as by paying compensation to repair the damage caused by the crime.

■ Marxists see punishment as serving the interests of capitalism by maintaining the existing capitalist social order and keeping the workers under control. **Althusser** (1971) argues that punishment is part of the **repressive state apparatus** that, along with the police and the CJS, is used to uphold the interests of the capitalist class, e.g. the protection of private property. Just like the law, Marxists would argue that punishment is selectivity enforced. **Rusche and Kirchheimer** (1939) argue that as the interests of the ruling class change, so do the forms of punishment. The introduction of prisons was useful in early capitalism for training workers to the discipline of long hours in alienating and poor working conditions and to deal with periods of high unemployment.

■ Despite New Labour's emphasis on being 'tough on the causes of crime', it agreed with the right realist approach of the Conservatives that there should be a strong emphasis on punishment. Subsequently, since the 1980s the UK prison population has steadily increased (from 60,000 in 1997 to 86,000 in 2015). **Garland** (2001) described the reliance on prisons as a form of punishment as an era of '**mass incarceration**' and in the USA this applied particularly to young black males. However, the high rates of **recidivism** (repeat offending) suggest that prison as a policy of crime control and prevention does not work. For the two-thirds of prisoners who reoffend, prison clearly fails to act as a deterrent or perform the function of rehabilitation. Garland suggests that in the late-modern period the failure of such policies has led governments to be more concerned with creating the perception that they are managing rather than preventing crime (such as referring to official statistics that crime rates are falling).

■ **Surveillance** as a form of social control and crime control has been expanding quietly for many decades and is now a growing feature of modern life. **Foucault** (1977) argues that the nature of social control (or discipline, as he refers to it) has changed from public punishments to the body, such as executions, to more subtle forms of punishment, particularly in late modernity. As well as being carried out by a greater range of agents of social control than just the police, punishments now seek to control the mind as well as the body. Foucault argues that this **disciplinary power** is achieved though surveillance, which he felt was illustrated by the **panopticon** (meaning 'all-seeing place') whereby the design of the prison allowed guards to watch prisoners in their cells without being seen. This resulted in a form of **self-surveillance** — the prisoners would behave as they had no way of knowing whether the guards were watching them.

■ **Cohen** (1985) agrees with Foucault's idea that social control has now spread to more agents of social control, such as youth offending workers and even schools and private companies. Cohen (in Innes, 2003) argues that as a result of the increase in community-based controls such as antisocial behaviour orders (ASBOs), the CJS and the authorities have been able to cast the '**net of control**' over more people. Like Foucault, Cohen argues that this has led to the use of more subtle controls such as CCTV, electronic tagging and curfews. This links to the increased use of surveillance in crime control in the late-modern era.

Knowledge check 13

What did Foucault mean by disciplinary power?

Liquid surveillance

- In the late-modern (or postmodern) era societies are more 'fluid' and their citizens, who are always on the move, are continually monitored, tracked and traced through CCTV, passwords and coded controls on buildings. **Bauman and Lyon** (2013) argue that this **liquid surveillance** is flexible and mobile and is spreading into more areas of life:

  1 As travellers — passport control with body scanners and biometric checks, chips in passports, checking-in by smartphone

  2 As consumers — strategies such as monitoring searches and cookies, customer databases, using smartphones to scan QR (quick response) codes or when purchasing goods

  3 As users of social media — by exchanging personal information such as personal profiles

- Whereas surveillance used to be solid and more fixed, such as in prisons, Bauman argues that it is now **post-panoptical**, the 'watchers' no longer need to be present and can escape beyond reach. While the details of our daily lives become more transparent to the organisations watching us, their activities become increasingly difficult to discern. In terms of social media, the loss of personal data to 'friends' illustrates how individual security may have to be sacrificed by individuals in order to partake in the 'cyberworld'.

- Bauman and Lyon argue that the key metaphor for liquid surveillance is 'big brother' and that power can now move with the 'speed of an electrical button'. They argue that as well as privacy, liquid surveillance also involves issues of justice and human rights. They point to how 'Arabs and Muslims' are subjected to more 'random' security checks at airports than other groups. They also argue that the ever-increasing use of drone surveillance can be abused by powerful groups and nations and provides no shelter for those spied upon.

> **Exam tip**
>
> Be prepared to link topics of state crime and cybercrime to a question on social control, crime and surveillance. In terms of state crime, the use of drones in the 'war on terror' and air strikes in countries such as Syria are viewed by some as war crimes.

Victimisation

There are two main sociological theories that explain how people become victims of crime.

- **Positivist victimology** As suggested by **Miers** (1989), positivist victimology focuses on interpersonal crimes of violence, attempts to identify the factors that produce patterns in victimisation and explains how victims have contributed to their own victimisaton. In relation to the latter, factors have been identified, such as low intelligence and how actions such as being the first person to use violence can lead to victimisation. Positivist victimology has been criticised for victim blaming and failing to examine less visible crime, such as state and green crime.

- **Critical (or radical) victimology** This criticises positivist victimology for failing to take account of structural inequalities. **Mawby and Walklate** (1994) argue that victimisation is a form of structural powerlessness. Just as with crime, critical victimology argues that the idea of being a victim is socially constructed. **Christie** (1986) states that the stereotypical 'ideal victim' in society is generally weak, innocent and blameless and is the target of an attack by a stranger. Critical criminology points to how the CJS can deny a victim their status by not applying the label of victim. **Tombs and White** (2007) have pointed to the ideological nature of this. For example, by failing to press charges against employers for industrial injury, the crimes of capitalism remain hidden. Similarly, feminists argue that by not pressing charges in cases of domestic violence, the crime stays invisible and women are denied the status of victim and the right to any redress. Positivist victimology would criticise critical victimology for failing to acknowledge that victims bring their victimisation on themselves.

Patterns of victimisation

1 Men are almost twice as likely to become victims of violent crime than women, despite women having a greater fear of crime.

2 Women are more likely to be the victims of domestic violence and sexual attacks than men.

3 Young males aged between 16 and 24 experience most violent crime.

4 Ethnic minorities, particularly mixed race, are more likely to be at risk of being a victim of crime than whites.

5 The poorest groups, such as the unemployed and the homeless, are more likely to be victims of crime than other social groups.

Knowledge check 14

Outline two criticisms of positivist victimology.

Summary

After studying this section, you should be aware of types of crime control, surveillance, prevention and punishment, victims, and the role of the criminal justice system and other agencies. You should be familiar with the following:

■ right and left realist crime prevention strategies

■ sociological explanations of the role of punishment, the criminal justice system and other agencies such as prisons

■ surveillance as a form of social and crime control, including liquid surveillance

■ positivist and critical victimology and patterns of victimisation

Theory and methods

For sociological research methods, which you will have studied in Year 1, refer to Student Guide 1 (see pages 27–40.)

■ Consensus, conflict, structural and social action theories

Functionalism

- Functionalism is a 'macro', large-scale structural theory that tends to use **positivist** methods to understand society and uncover the impact of social forces on individuals' behaviour. Durkheim (1897), who laid the foundations for modern functionalism, used a scientific approach to demonstrate how suicide was a social fact caused by factors external to the individual (see the section on sociology as a science).
- Parsons (1951) developed Durkheim's ideas into a systematic theory of society. The starting point is the **organic analogy**. Just like a living organism, society is made of **interconnected** and **interdependent** parts. Just as different parts of the body, such as the heart and brain, must work together to bring about good health, so different institutions, such as the family and the education system, must work together to bring about and maintain social order.
- Parsons argues that society has four basic needs (or **functional prerequisites**) that are met by four different **subsystems**:
  1 **Adaptation** Society has to provide a basic standard of living. Subsystem: economic, through institutions such as factories and the banking system.
  2 **Goal attainment** Society has to have decision-making procedures. Subsystem: political, through institutions such as political parties.
  3 **Integration** Society must develop institutions to ensure shared goals and reduce conflict. Subsystems: education, religion and the media.
  4 **Latency** Relates to how individuals are able to cope with society over time. Subsystem: kinship, though institutions such as the family. Parsons divided latency into **pattern maintenance**, such as families socialising their members into acceptable forms of behaviour and roles, and **tension management**, which ensures people are motivated to perform their roles and not oppose society.
- Functionalism argues that in order for the various parts of society to work together there must be **value consensus**. Basic norms and values, such as basic manners, are passed down through **primary socialisation** in the family while agents of **secondary socialisation**, such as the education system, socialise children into the wider culture and values of achievement and competition that are required in the workplace. In addition to socialisation, value consensus and social integration

are also achieved though **social control**. This can occur through informal **agencies** of social control, such as the family using positive sanctions such as rewards, or through punishments administered by **formal agencies** of social control such as the criminal justice system.

- Both Durkheim and Parsons argue that industrialisation led to a change from a **traditional** to a **modern** society. Parsons argues that different **pattern variables** (typical patterns of norms) exist in each society. The pattern variables that existed in traditional societies, such as collective orientation and ascribed status (i.e. status fixed at birth), were replaced in a modern society by individualism and achieved status. However, functionalists believe that social change is **evolutionary**. Parsons argues that a process of **structural differentiation** occurs whereby institutions gradually develop to meet the needs of society. For example, in a modern society some of the functions performed by the kinship system, such as providing skills for future jobs, have been taken over by other institutions such as the education system.

Merton — an internal critique

- Merton (1957), a functionalist, argues that Parsons was wrong to assume that all institutions were functional for all parts of society. He argues that some institutions could be **dysfunctional** for society, such as religion leading to conflict and division in society. Merton also disagrees with Parsons that all institutions, such as the nuclear family, are **functionally indispensable**. He argues that there may be **functional alternatives**, such as same-sex parents being able to fulfil the function of effective socialisation. Merton feels that Parson's analysis of society is too simplistic. For example, not all institutions are interdependent and there may be **latent** (hidden) functions as well as **manifest** (intended) ones.

Evaluation

- + Functionalism shows the macro influence of society over the individual.
- + Value consensus does exist in society. Different institutions do work together.
- – Functionalists such as Durkheim were not as scientific as is claimed. For example, he did not operationalise concepts such as integration in his study of suicide.
- – **Marxists** argue that functionalists ignore conflict and differences in power in society.
- – **Interactionists** and **postmodernists** argue that people are more reflexive and are not puppets whose actions are determined by pattern variables such as universalistic norms in schools (illustrated by students' rejecting teacher labels).
- – **Postmodernism** regards functionalism as a **metanarrative** that cannot explain the diversity that exists in values in society today.
- – **Conflict theorists** and **postmodernists** would argue that functionalism over-emphasises the level of consensus in society. For example, feminists claim that, as well as ignoring patriarchy, functionalists fail to explain differing attitudes towards gender roles in society today.
- – Functionalists' view of social change is criticised, particularly by **Marxists**, who argue that change can be revolutionary as well as evolutionary.

Exam tip

To illustrate general functionalist ideas, be prepared to refer to topic areas such as education. For example, while Durkheim argued that the teaching of history would help develop social solidarity and a sense of belonging to society, Parsons felt that education acted as a bridge between the particularistic values of the home and the universalistic values of the workplace.

Marxism

- Like functionalism, Marxism is a macro, structural perspective that attempts to study the influence of social institutions over individuals in a scientific manner. Rather than it being based on consensus, however, Marx argued that capitalist society is based on conflict between two social classes, the **bourgeoisie** (Bs), who own the means of production, and the **proletariat** (Ps), who are the working class who hire out their labour in return for a wage. The Bs seek to maximise profits, or surplus value, by exploiting the Ps, leading to inequalities in income and wealth. Marx argued that this inequality would increase over time and lead to a polarisation of the classes, which would eventually lead to revolution.

- Marx argued that because the Bs owned the **infrastructure** (the economic base) of society, they were able to have control over other institutions in society contained in the **superstructure**, such as the family, religion, the media and the education system. The function of the superstructure was to pass on ruling-class ideology to the Ps and help **reproduce** and **legitimise** the inequalities that existed in a capitalist society. As a result, the Ps are lulled into a **false class consciousness** as they are 'brainwashed' into believing that capitalism is fair and are unable to see through the oppression they suffer. Marx argued that eventually the Ps would become a '**class for itself**' and wake up to the exploitation and inequality they faced and collectively overthrow capitalism and replace it with a classless **communist** society.

Means of production The things required in the process of production that can be owned, such as land, machinery, tools and factories (but not labour).

Surplus value The difference between the value of goods produced and wages paid by capitalists.

Polarisation Due to continued exploitation in capitalism, the rich will get richer and the poor will get poorer.

Exam tip

Be prepared to link other topics you have studied to explain the Marxist view of legitimation and reproduction. For example, discuss how Marxists Bowles and Gintis' concepts of the myth of meritocracy and the hidden curriculum can be used to examine class inequality in the education system. Similarly, the policy of the minimum wage would be viewed by Marxists as an ideological tool which justifies and legitimates low pay and exploitation while seemingly showing the caring face of capitalism.

- Like Durkheim, Marx felt society should be studied in a scientific way. He described his theory as 'scientific socialism'. This can be seen in his theory of social change, referred to as historical materialism. He argues that the nature of class conflict and exploitation that exists between two social groups in every epoch or time period changes over time. For example, in ancient society it was based on slavery, which changed to the ownership of land in the feudal period. Marx's 'hypothesis' was that after the proletariat revolution, there would be the establishment of the last epoch, communism, which would lead to an end to the exploitation and alienation that existed in capitalism.

Historical materialism A way of studying developed by Marx of how human societies collectively produce the necessities of life over time.

Alienation A feeling of a lack of control resulting from living in a society stratified into social classes. For example, on a factory assembly line, workers feel little job satisfaction due to a lack of input into the process of production.

Exam tip

Develop analysis by comparing the similarities and differences between functionalism and Marxism. For example, compare Marx's view that there are two key social institutions (with one, the infrastructure, controlling the other for the benefit of one group) with Parson's view that there are four subsystems working harmoniously for the benefit of all society.

Evaluation

+ Marxism explains inequality in society. Exploitation in the workplace does occur.
+ It shows how society, particularly economic factors, influences individuals.
+ It provides an explanation for how conflict in society developed over time.
- **Functionalists** would argue that there is too much emphasis on conflict and that there are examples of capitalism benefiting all society, such as the welfare state and improvements in the standard of living. They argue shared values do exist and that there is consensus in society.
- The revolution that Marx predicted has not occurred; capitalism has grown stronger and, as a result of globalisation, has spread across the world.
- When communist regimes have been established they have been unsuccessful, such as in China and the USSR. Marxists would counter this by arguing that they were not truly communist states.
- The polarisation of the classes has not occurred. As **Weber** argues, the middle classes have increased considerably, contrary to what Marx predicted.
- **Feminists** argue that Marxists ignore gender inequality, such as the gender pay gap.
- **Social action theorists** argue that Marxism ignores the influence of the individual on society.

Neo-Marxism

■ Neo-Marxists **Althusser** and **Gramsci** are critical of the economic determinism of traditional Marxism and both develop the theory of ideology. Gramsci, to an extent, adopts a micro, social action approach and argues that individual ideas could exist independently of both the infrastructure and superstructure. He argues that the Ps are able to some extent to see through the dominant ideology and could challenge the hegemony of the Bs and bring about social change.

■ Althusser adopts a macro, structural approach and argues that it is not people's actions but conflicts within the social structure, between economic, political and ideological levels, that will lead to social change. Althusser argues that there are two ways through which the state reproduces capitalism: **repressive state apparatuses** (RSAs) such as the police and prisons, and **ideological state apparatuses** (ISAs) such as education and the media.

■ **The Frankfurt School** refers to other neo-Marxist sociologists who developed Marxist theory. Marcuse (1964) argued that Marx did not take account of the key role that the media play in shaping and manipulating our needs, e.g. through advertising. He argued that the media also divert the attention of the working class away from the injustices of capitalism by promoting trivial forms of entertainment, as seen in 'reality' TV programmes today.

■ A different type of neo-Marxism using a **postmodern** framework is developed by **Harvey** (1990). He argues that, since the 1970s, capitalism has moved into a different stage as a result of factors such as **globalisation** and the move in the economy from manufacturing to the service sector. This has led to what Harvey

> **Hegemony** The ideas and values of the ruling class that become the dominant view in society. These are transmitted via institutions such as the media, education and religion.

Table 7 A comparison of two neo-Marxist views

Gramsci — humanist		Althusser — structuralist
Humans have free will and are active. People's conscious ideas can lead to social change	Disagree	This is an illusion. Macro, structural factors will cause social change. People are puppets controlled by ideology
The working class can become class conscious and can see through dominant ideology	Disagree	This is a false consciousness constructed by ISAs — e.g. the myth of meritocracy in education
Working-class protests can lead to change — the proletariat can construct a counter-hegemonic bloc of leadership based on socialist principles	Disagree	The crisis in capitalism can lead to change as a result of contradictions between the three structures: economic, political and ideological
Coercion — force Ps to accept the rule of the Bs via the police, the army and the courts	Agree	RSAs — these coerce the Ps to comply with the will of the Bs
Consent — the media, religion, education etc. persuade the Ps to accept the ruling class rule as legitimate	Agree	ISAs — these ideologically manipulate the Ps to see capitalism as legitimate
Rejects economic determinism of Marx	Agree	Rejects economic determinism of Marx

calls '**flexible accumulation**'. This involves new ways of achieving profits, such as: exploiting the labour power in developing countries to produce cheap goods, the requirement of a more flexible workforce such as being on zero-hour contracts, and technologically-based products such as tablets and mobile phones. Harvey points to other effects of these changes on capitalism, such as transnational companies being more important than nation-states, and gender, ethnicity and religion replacing social class as the main forms of division and inequality in society.

Social action theory

- Social action theories reject structural, macro theories and argue that society is constructed through people's interactions and meanings (such as in the labelling process). Theories such as **symbolic interactionism** (the full name for interactionism) are micro, small-scale theories that tend to use interpretivist methods and reject the positivist approach adopted by structural theories. Social action theory argues that individuals, rather than being controlled like puppets by the nature of capitalist society (as Marxists argue) or pattern variables (as Parsons suggests), make their own choices and that society is constructed from people's meanings and interpretations. For example, while social roles such as teacher and student exist, they are only guidelines which individuals can interpret and negotiate with others.
- While accepting the significance of objective, causal, structural factors, **Weber** (1905) argued that the role of the sociologist was to uncover **verstehen** — the subjective meanings that individuals attach to their behaviour. He argued that interpretivist methods were needed to understand social action.
- **Symbolic interactionism** (SI) refers to the process whereby people acquire knowledge about what is appropriate behaviour in different social situations. **Mead** (1934) argued that the world is composed of many different symbols, which are not fixed but have meanings which shape our behaviour. For example, a kiss can be interpreted and responded to differently depending on the context in which it

Knowledge check 15

Outline two areas of agreement between Gramsci and Althusser.

occurs. On a first date the response to a kiss would be very different to a kiss when greeting a relative at a funeral.

- **Blumer** (1962) argues that as children we develop the notion of the **self**, which is partly due to how an individual interprets their experiences, such as learning social roles through playing games, but also is a product of how others see us. **Cooley** (1922) developed the idea of the **looking-glass self** to describe how we learn to see ourselves as others see us.

- Labelling theory developed from SI and was applied by **Becker** (1961) to study how agents of social control, such as teachers and the police, are able to apply negative labels in the process of interaction. These labels, applied in education or policing, can have a negative impact on the self-esteem and status of those labelled, often leading to a **self-fulfilling prophecy** where the label is accepted (see the Interactionism: labelling theory section). **Goffman's** (1963) **dramaturgical** approach is a version of SI which argues that social interaction is like a play in which the roles of the 'actors' are only loosely 'scripted' by society.

- Unlike SI, which accepts the influence of the social structure, such as the influence of social class on educational achievement or offending, **phenomenologists** argue that society is not 'real' but socially constructed. Social class is a phenomenon that is 'made up' by society. **Schultz** (1899–1959) argues that members of society use a set of shared categories or '**typifications**' to make sense of the world and clarify any meanings that are unclear. Schultz argues that these typifications or common-sense knowledge give the impression that the world is ordered but in fact it is socially constructed.

- These ideas were developed by **ethnomethodologist Garfinkel** (1967), who argued that rather than explaining the effects of meaning (such as the way coroners label deaths), sociologists should study the methods that are used to produce meanings in the first place, i.e. how actors create meanings. Garfinkel argues that we use reflexivity to make sense of the world when there is confusion over the meanings of certain behaviours. For example, coroners make sense of the confusion over the cause of death by using their common-sense knowledge of 'facts' about suicide cases, such as the mental health of the deceased or their marital status.

Exam tip

Be prepared to apply the ideas of Garfinkel and phenomenologists such as Atkinson to the debate as to whether sociology is a science. They totally reject Durkheim's positivist, scientific approach and argue that the official statistics that are used to explain suicide are socially constructed. They would argue that these statistics tell us more about the common-sense assumptions of coroners and cannot be used to make 'laws' about the causes of suicide.

- **Giddens** (1984) combines theories of structure and social action in his theory of **structuration**. He argues that while individuals are restricted by structural factors such as norms, customs and laws, they have choice and can respond to these factors in different ways. Giddens argues that increasingly in a late-modern society (see the section on modernity and post-modernism) social structures are open to change by the actions of individuals.

Exam tip

Be prepared to discuss the differences between the various social action approaches. While labelling theory has been criticised for seeing the individual as passively accepting labels, Goffman argues that through impression management individuals actively seek to present themselves in a way they wish others to see them.

Reflexivity The use of common-sense knowledge to make sense of social reality.

Evaluation

- + Social action theory, with its emphasis on interpretivist methodology, has provided a rich insight into the interaction process in small-scale settings.
- + Social action theories are voluntaristic; they demonstrate how people have free will and are able to shape society.
- + Social action theories such as interactionism avoid the deterministic nature of structural theories such as Marxism and functionalism.
- – **Structural theories** argue that social action theory fails to take account of the wider social context in which interaction takes place. It fails to explain the origins of labels and symbolic meanings.
- – **Functionalists** argue that social action theory ignores the influence of consistent patterns, such as shared norms, that influence people's behaviour. Ethnomethodology, in particular, has been criticised for denying the existence of a wider society.
- – **Marxists** and **feminists** argue that social action theory fails to fully explore the power differences between individuals and social groups in society. Becker does respond to this criticism and argues that labelling theory does examine the power relationship between those labelled and the agents of social control.
- – Giddens' structuration theory has been criticised by **Marxists** for over-estimating the extent to which individuals can change social structures.

> **Knowledge check 16**
>
> What is the difference between phenomenology and symbolic interactionism?

Feminism

Like Marxism, feminism is a conflict theory that tends to adopt a structuralist approach. However, feminists argue that inequalities are based on **patriarchy**, or male dominance, rather than on social class. Feminism seeks to show how social institutions such as the family, education and media can contribute to the oppression of women. While quantitative data would be used to show structural patterns of gender inequality, such as the pay gap, most feminist research is qualitative and interpretivist in nature. For example, **Dobash and Dobash** (1979) used informal, unstructured interviews in order to gain an understanding of the experiences of women who had been the victims of domestic violence. Feminism is critical of traditional sociology for being **malestream**, as it ignores the viewpoint of women. There are three main types of feminist theory (see Table 8).

Further evaluation points on feminist theories

- + Liberal feminists would argue that Marxist feminists and radical feminists fail to recognise how women's position has improved as a result of changes in legislation and attitudes to gender roles.
- + **Dual systems** feminists such as Hartman (1979) criticise Marxist feminism and liberal feminism for being too simplistic and argue that capitalism and patriarchy are intertwined to form 'patriarchal capitalism'.
- – Due to its structural nature, feminism can be accused of being over-deterministic. It does not take account of how individual females may interpret their situation. As **Hakim** (2000) argues, not all women feel oppressed by being housewives and mothers.

> **Reserve army of labour**
> A Marxist concept to explain how groups, such as women, can be brought into the labour market when there is a shortage of workers. When there is a boom in a capitalist economy they will be hired; when there is a recession they will be the first to be fired.

Table 8 Feminist theories

	Liberal feminism (LF) — Oakley (1974)	Marxist feminism (MF) — Barrett (1980)	Radical feminism (RF) — Firestone (1972)
What is the problem?	Lack of opportunities in education, employment and politics. Women's oppression has been maintained through sexist **gender socialisation** — e.g. the belief that the housewife–mother role is the primary role for women	**Capitalism** with its patriarchal ideology controls and exploits women in a number of ways: ■ the unpaid role of housewife, which nurtures the current and next generation of workers ■ absorbing the anger of male workers, e.g. domestic violence ■ part of the **reserve army of labour**	Men are the 'enemy'. **Patriarchy** exists in all areas of society. Due to childbirth, women are dependent on men, who oppress and exploit them in all areas of life, from sexual relations in the home to discrimination in the workplace
How should it be solved?	Society's socialisation patterns must be changed, such as positive female role models in the media The introduction of legislation to combat gender discrimination, such as the Equal Pay Act LFs argue that the **feminisation** of education and the economy provides evidence that women's opportunities are improving	Capitalism must be overthrown for women to be free from oppression and patriarchy. It is the main cause of women's oppression Barrett argues that the ideology of '**familism**' must also be overthrown. This promotes the idea to women that they should accept and be satisfied with their role as housewife–mother within the nuclear family	Revolutionary change: ■ **Separation** Some RFs argue that women must live separately from men in order to break free from the threat of male violence and sexual aggression ■ **Political lesbianism** Other RFs argue that lesbianism is the only way in which women can escape male oppression in personal and sexual relationships
Strengths	LFs are arguably correct to argue that changes in gender socialisation and legislation have led to a decrease in gender inequality	MFs are right to draw attention to the impact of capitalism on gender inequality. As well as the pay gap, males dominate the top positions in the economy	RF has demonstrated how female oppression occurs in the private sphere of the domestic and sexual relationships
Weaknesses	MF and RF would argue that LF exaggerates the progress made and ignores the continuing influence of capitalism and patriarchy on gender inequality. The Equal Pay Act has not led to equal pay for women	Not all women are part of a reserve army of labour and this theory also fails to explain why some jobs are dominated by women or why women end up being responsible for domestic labour. MF fails to explain gender inequality in non-capitalist societies	RF has been criticised for being too extreme, e.g. in seeing all men as the enemy. Its solutions of separation and political lesbianism are unrealistic. MF argues that it is class and not patriarchy that is the real cause of women's oppression

- **Difference feminists** would argue that theories such as liberal feminism which argue that patriarchy is universal are failing to acknowledge that women are not a homogeneous group. The experiences of women will be influenced by a range of factors such as social class, ethnicity, religion, age.
- **Black feminists** agree and argue that forms of feminism that strive to overcome patriarchy and class oppression but ignore ethnicity can discriminate against women through racial bias.
- **Postmodern feminists** also agree that previous feminist theories fail to reflect the diversity of the experiences of women and that terms such as patriarchy do not affect all women in the same way. Like all modern theorists, postmodernists regard feminism as a metanarrative.

Exam tip

Exam tip

If you are asked to evaluate the usefulness of feminist theories in understanding society, be prepared to discuss the strengths and weaknesses of the different types of feminism. When evaluating feminist theories you should also refer to how they relate to other sociological theories, e.g. the agreement between Marxism and Marxist feminists.

Exam tip

As well as the methodological approach used by feminists, be prepared to link topic areas to a question on feminism, such as improvement in educational achievement to support the liberal feminist view or the use of 'sex to sell' in gender portrayal in the media to support the Marxist feminist arguments.

■ Modernity and postmodernism

- The industrial revolution which led to urbanisation, capitalism and the development of nation-states led to the start of modernity, or modern society. **Modern theories** such as Marxism, functionalism and positivism were part of the **Enlightenment project** — the belief that knowledge and rational, scientific thinking could lead to progress in society. For example, positivist sociology rejected traditional sources of knowledge such as religion and argued that a scientific approach was needed to explain how the modern world worked and could be improved.

- **Postmodernists** argue, however, that the rapid social and economic changes that occurred in the later part of the twentieth century (from around the late 1970s) have led to the end of the modern era. Significant aspects of a postmodern society, often based on globalisation, include:

   1 a shift from **Fordist** mass production to a **post-Fordist** economy based on the service sector, technology and the need for a flexible workforce

   2 the decline of traditional sources of identity, particularly social class. These have been replaced by the consumption of consumer goods, notably global brands such as Nike and Apple

   3 life in a media-saturated society where popular culture shapes personal identity through satellite TV and, increasingly, the internet and mobile phones

- Postmodernist **Lyotard** (1984) argues that contemporary society cannot be explained by metanarratives, such as Marxism and functionalism, as it is based on isolated individuals who are linked by a few social bonds, rather than being controlled by structural factors.

- **Baudrillard** (1983) agreed that individuals were largely isolated and argued that the increasing consumption of the media to experience the world has led to the 'death of the social'. He also argued that we consume commodities as a sign or way of expressing ourselves rather than for the function that they perform. He developed the idea of **simulacra**, meaning that media images that are not based on reality, such as 'celebrities', are increasingly used to model our behaviour. The media also create a world of **hyperreality**, where people cannot distinguish image from reality — e.g. the belief that 'celebrities' such as Keith Lemon are real.

- Rather than society moving to a new set of economic and social circumstances as postmodernists argue, **late modernists** see the rapid social changes that have recently occurred as a continuation of modern society. Late-modernist theorists such as **Giddens** (1984) and **Beck** (1992) agree with postmodernists that factors such as increasing individualism and globalisation are causing new problems for society. However, they share the view of the Enlightenment project that these problems can be addressed and that reason can be used to improve society.

- Part of Giddens' **structuration theory** (see the section on social action theory) was that there is a **duality of structure**; that people (or 'agents' as Giddens refers to them) could 'make' society as well as being influenced by it. He argues that people engage in **reflexivity**, whereby they constantly monitor their own situation in the light of information and seek change if needed.
- Beck agrees with Giddens and argues that the complex changes of the late-modern period, such as global warming and an unstable economy, have led to what he calls a **risk society**. He argues that individuals are more aware of these ever-increasing risks and use reflexivity to take action to reduce them. This can range from joining political movements such as the 'War on Poverty' to improving lifestyles by changing eating habits.

Evaluation

+ Late modernists and postmodernists are right to draw attention to the inadequacies of modern theories in explaining recent changes in society, such as the impact of factors such as globalisation.
+ Postmodernists are right to argue that there is greater diversity and choice in society and that people are able to 'pick and mix' their own identity via the media and the consumption of cultural products.
- **Modern theories** would argue that the ability to make these choices and consume is dependent on factors such as social class, gender and ethnicity.
- **Conflict theories** criticise postmodernists for ignoring the significance of structural factors and how gender and class shape people's life chances and identity.
- **Social action theory** argues that postmodernism ignores interactions between individuals and that people are active and able to distinguish between fiction and reality.
- Postmodernism is critical of sociological theories for not offering the 'truth' — but why should we accept their view of society as accurate?
- Beck has been criticised for ignoring the fact that risks faced may be influenced by factors such as social class and that some individuals may not have the power to be able to use reflexivity to reduce these risks.
- Postmodernists reject the view of late modernists that the 'risks' of society can be reduced by reflexivity.

■ The relationship between sociological theory and methods

Figure 1, on page 42, provides an overview of the relationship between theory and methods. *Refer to Student Guide 1 for sociological research methods (pages 27–40).*

Exam tip

Be prepared to compare Giddens' use of reflexivity with social action theory. Giddens develops the symbolic interactionist notion of taking the role of the other as, through reflexivity, individuals are able to see themselves as others see them and create their own identity. Ethnomethodologists argue that reflexivity is not just used to shape our own identities but is used to make sense of reality and social order itself.

Exam tip

In evaluating the postmodern and late-modern views, be prepared to discuss the views of Harvey and the Marxist version of how capitalism has developed after the modern era (see the Neo-Marxism section).

Knowledge check 17

Outline two strengths of postmodern theory.

Theory and methods

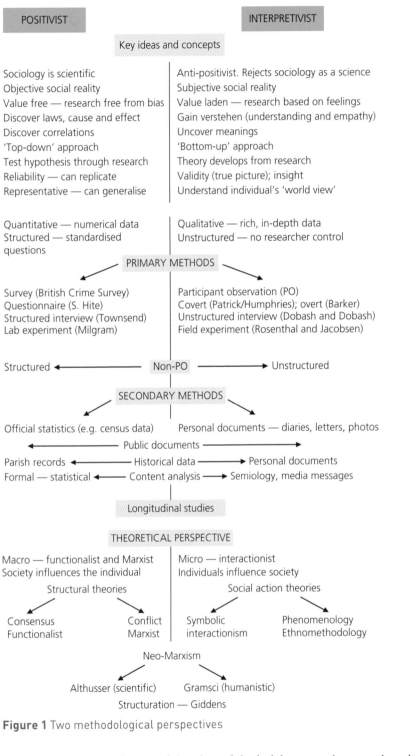

POSITIVIST **INTERPRETIVIST**

Key ideas and concepts

Sociology is scientific	Anti-positivist. Rejects sociology as a science
Objective social reality	Subjective social reality
Value free — research free from bias	Value laden — research based on feelings
Discover laws, cause and effect	Gain verstehen (understanding and empathy)
Discover correlations	Uncover meanings
'Top-down' approach	'Bottom-up' approach
Test hypothesis through research	Theory develops from research
Reliability — can replicate	Validity (true picture); insight
Representative — can generalise	Understand individual's 'world view'

Quantitative — numerical data
Structured — standardised questions

Qualitative — rich, in-depth data
Unstructured — no researcher control

PRIMARY METHODS

Survey (British Crime Survey)
Questionnaire (S. Hite)
Structured interview (Townsend)
Lab experiment (Milgram)

Participant observation (PO)
Covert (Patrick/Humphries); overt (Barker)
Unstructured interview (Dobash and Dobash)
Field experiment (Rosenthal and Jacobsen)

Structured ◄——————— Non-PO ———————► Unstructured

SECONDARY METHODS

Official statistics (e.g. census data)   Personal documents — diaries, letters, photos

◄——————— Public documents ———————►

Parish records ◄——————— Historical data ———————► Personal documents
Formal — statistical ◄——— Content analysis ———► Semiology, media messages

Longitudinal studies

THEORETICAL PERSPECTIVE

Macro — functionalist and Marxist
Society influences the individual
Structural theories

Micro — interactionist
Individuals influence society
Social action theories

Consensus
Functionalist

Conflict
Marxist

Symbolic
interactionism

Phenomenology
Ethnomethodology

Neo-Marxism

Althusser (scientific)   Gramsci (humanistic)
Structuration — Giddens

Figure 1 Two methodological perspectives

While this chart provides a useful outline of the link between theory and method it is to a certain extent artificial as researchers' choice of method may be influenced by a variety of factors including practical and ethical issues. A **longitudinal study**, rather than being a specific method, is when the researcher follows the same sample over an extended period and conducts research at set intervals, e.g. every 5 years. **Positivists** would favour the use of questionnaires to gain statistics so correlations over time could be measured and causes identified. An **interpretivist** would see the benefit of longitudinal research being that it provides more than just a one-off snapshot and would favour the use of unstructured interviews to examine developments over time. However, for both types of approach a researcher would face some practical problems of longitudinal research. It is costly, takes time to get results and faces sample attrition, where people may drop out of the study, meaning that the sample may become less representative.

Summary

After studying these sections, you should be aware of consensus, conflict, structural and social action theories, the concepts of modernity and postmodernity in relation to sociological theory, and the relationship between theory and methods. You should be familiar with the following:

- the difference between consensus theories, e.g. functionalism, and conflict theories, e.g. different Marxist and feminist theories
- the difference between structural theories, e.g. functionalism and Marxism, and action theories,

e.g. symbolic interactionism, phenomenology and ethnomethodology

- attempts to combine structural and action theories such as structuration and humanist neo-Marxism
- modern, late-modern and postmodern theories of contemporary society
- the relationship between methodological approaches of positivism and interpretivism and sociological theory

Sociology as a science

Positivism versus interpretivism

- Positivists such as **Durkheim** argue that sociology can and should model itself on the natural sciences and use quantitative methods to study society objectively.
- Positivists argue that sociologists can discover laws about human behaviour by using the **hypothetico-deductive model**. This goes through the following stages: the researcher observes something, thinks of a hypothesis to explain it, gathers data through systematic observation and measurement, establishes a law to show how the evidence supports the hypothesis. The process of **verification**, checking something is true, should be used to prove or refute a hypothesis.
- Positivists believe that as it is possible for sociologists to study social phenomena objectively, value freedom is possible as the researcher's own beliefs will not influence how they conduct their research or interpret their results.
- Durkheim used the **comparative method**, comparing suicide statistics to discover laws of cause and effect on suicide. He believed that patterns in suicide rates were caused by differences in social integration and moral regulation. This he discovered by examining correlations in the suicide rates and other variables such as the religion of different European counties. Suicide rates were social facts, caused by the structure of the society, and were external to the individual.

- **Gibbs and Martin** argue that Durkheim was not scientific as he did not operationalise concepts such as social integration.
- Interpretivists and social action theorists reject the claim that sociology can be an objective science. They argue that the purpose of sociological inquiry is to uncover meanings and gain verstehen through qualitative methods, not to establish cause and effect. They would argue that sociologists, rather than being value free and objective, need to be subjective and will inevitably be influenced by their values.
- Interactionist **Douglas** (1967) rejects Durkheim's use of official statistics to make laws on suicide. Douglas argues that suicide statistics, rather than being scientific and objective, are based on the subjective opinions of coroners. Their verdicts may be influenced by factors such as relatives not wanting a suicide verdict to bring shame on their family, particularly in a Catholic country.
- Ethnomethodologist **Atkinson** (1978) argues that suicide is an individual act, not a social fact. Official statistics on suicide are socially constructed — they say more about the interpretations of coroners than levels of suicide. Interactionists believe that by using a '**bottom-up**' approach, sociologists can develop theories such as labelling being based on 'macro' factors such as social class. However, ethnomethodologists totally reject causal explanations of human behaviour. They argue that there are no macro, structural explanations for social phenomena that can be studied in a scientific way as positivists suggest.

Views on the nature of science

- **Popper** rejects the hypothetico-deductive approach of positivism and argues that scientific knowledge should be based on the process of **falsification** (that it can be proved wrong) rather than verification. Popper feels that while sociology could be scientific, as it can produce a hypothesis that can be tested, most sociology is unscientific as it cannot be proved wrong.
- **Kuhn** (1962) argues that scientific knowledge works within a shared framework agreed by members, which he refers to as a **paradigm**. He rejects the views of science held by positivists and Popper and argues that there is no objective independent scientific knowledge. Rather, scientific knowledge works within paradigms, such as the Earth is flat, which will only change when enough evidence is found that does not support the paradigm. Kuhn argues that as sociology does not have a shared and dominant paradigm, due to various competing theories, it cannot be considered to be a science.
- **Feyerabend** (1975) is also critical of positivists and Popper and argues that individual scientists will bend the rules and 'tweak' data to prove their theories, rather than being objective and rational. There have been many examples of 'cheating' in science, such as Burt's research into three types of intelligence which formed the basis for the tripartite education system.
- **Realists** argue that like some natural scientists, such as meteorologists, sociologists have to study society in '**open systems**', where variables cannot necessarily be controlled and measured. Therefore, sociology can attempt to be scientific in studying open systems in a neutral way. Just like some natural sciences, sociology studies unobservable, underlying structures. For example, social class cannot be directly observed, but its impact, such as on educational attainment, can be measured.

Knowledge check 18

What is the difference between the views of Popper and the positivist view of science?

- There are therefore four main views on science:
  1. Positivist — prove theories by testing a hypothesis — verification
  2. Popper — prove other theories wrong — falsification
  3. Kuhn — scientific knowledge is based on paradigms — which offer explanations
  4. Realist — science studies open and closed systems — science is about the search for underlying causes of things
- **Postmodernists** such as **Lyotard** (1992) reject the idea of absolute truths and objectivity in knowledge. They argue that all knowledge is relative and that the view of science is just one version of the 'truth'. Postmodernists regard 'modern', positivist theories such as functionalism and Marxism as '**metanarratives**' ('big stories') that do not hold the 'truth' about society. They are out of date as they are no longer able to explain the diverse and fragmented nature of postmodern society.
- Postmodernism is criticised for being contradictory. Why should we believe postmodernism's version of 'the truth'?
- Similarly, some **feminists** argue that sociology should not attempt to be scientific. While some argue that no single scientific feminist theory could explain the experiences of all women, others argue that qualitative methods need to be used to gain understanding of the experiences of women.

Objectivity and values in sociology

- **Classical positivists** such as **Durkheim** argued that sociology could be value free. Sociologists should discover laws about human behaviour in order to understand how society works and to improve it through social policies. Positivists believe it is the job of the sociologist to establish the 'truth' in a neutral, detached way. Value freedom is possible as the researcher's own beliefs should not influence how they conduct their research or interpret their results.
- **Interpretivists** and social action theorists reject the claim that sociology can be an objective science. They argue that the purpose of sociological inquiry is to uncover meanings and gain verstehen through qualitative methods and not to establish cause and effect. They would argue that sociologists, rather than being value free and objective, need to be subjective and will inevitably be influenced by their values.
- **Weber** argues that sociologists cannot be value free when choosing a research topic and interpreting and applying findings. However, he feels that researchers should be objective and unbiased when carrying out their research.
- Modern positivists argue that sociologists can be value free as they can and should remain morally neutral when conducting research. Many sociologists such as Weber and **Gouldner** reject this view and argue that sociologists have a '**moral responsibility**' when conducting research. They argue that as citizens, researchers cannot divorce themselves from the potential harm that could result from the findings of their research.

> **Exam tip**
>
> Be prepared to apply issues from the sociology as a science debate to whether sociology can be value free. For example, realists argue that sociology can attempt to be scientific in studying open systems in a neutral way but they argue that sociologists cannot be completely value free.

> **Exam tip**
>
> An exam question may ask you to evaluate the claim that sociology can and/or should be value free. Make sure that arguments and evaluation points are clearly applied to these different claims.

- Gouldner also argued that sociologists should be 'committed' rather than 'morally neutral' and pretending to be value free. Sociologists such as **Marxists** and **feminists** argue that value freedom is undesirable and that sociologists should be **value laden** — they should make value judgements and should aim to improve society through sociological research.

- **Labelling theorist Becker** argues that sociologists should take the side of the 'underdog', such as working-class students and criminals labelled by powerful groups in society. Becker felt that interpretivist methods should be used to gain verstehen on the view of the 'outsiders'. Gouldner was critical of this as not going far enough. As a Marxist he argued that sociologists should be on the side of the people fighting back against capitalist society.

- For **postmodernists** all knowledge is relative; no one theory holds the absolute objective truth. All modern theories, such as Marxism and functionalism, are metanarratives and are based on values and assumptions. However, postmodernism could itself be described as being a metanarrative.

- Other factors may mean that sociologists cannot be value free in their research, e.g. who funds the research (such as governments not publishing findings it disagrees with) and sociologists' own careers (they may chose a popular topic to study that could further their career).

Summary

After studying these sections, you should be aware of the nature of science and the extent to which sociology can be regarded as scientific, and debates about subjectivity, objectivity and value freedom. You should be familiar with the following:
- debates about the scientific status of sociology: positivist and interpretivist views
- different views of the natural sciences, e.g. positivism, Popper, Kuhn and realism, and implications for sociology's scientific status
- postmodern and feminist views on sociology as a science
- different views on whether sociology can and should be objective or value free, e.g. classical sociology, value neutrality and committed sociology

Exam tip

Be prepared to relate methodological issues to the question of objectivity and value freedom. Interpretivist methods such as participant observation can lose objectivity if the researcher 'goes native'. While in 'objective' positivist methods such as questionnaires the researcher has imposed their own values on respondents by having pre-determined questions.

Knowledge check 19

What is the difference between value free and value laden?

■ Sociology and social policy

Worsley (1977) described a **social** problem as social behaviour such as juvenile delinquency that causes public and private misery and that requires a collective response, whereas a **sociological** problem is any pattern of behaviour that requires explanation. A sociological problem could be a social problem or 'normal' behaviour such as conforming to laws.

Social policies are parts of government policies that attempt to deal with social problems such as educational underachievement and crime. Social policy has been influenced by sociological perspectives and research in a variety of ways:

- In line with the Enlightenment project, **positivists** such as **Comte** and **Durkheim** saw sociological research as being crucial in combating social problems and improving society through rational thought. **Functionalists** agree and argue that the role of the sociologist is to provide the government with objective research findings based on positivist methodology. They argue that this information, such as research on educational achievement, can be used to inform social policies that will serve the interests of society as a whole.

- The **social democratic** perspective had a significant impact on the introduction of the welfare state after the Second World War. Later, Townsend's *Poverty in the United Kingdom* (1979) made recommendations to the government to change what he felt was an inadequate benefits system.

- Whereas the social democratic view argues that the state should redistribute wealth and income, the **New Right** view is that the state should have only a minimal involvement in society and that social policy can be the cause of social problems such as poverty. Researchers such as Marsland and his notion of the **dependency culture** influenced Conservative governments to cut back on welfare provision in the 1980s and beyond.

- Feminist theory and research has influenced government policies aimed at addressing gender inequality such as the GIST (Girls into Science and Technology) project in education and the Equal Pay Act. Whereas **liberal feminists** would argue such polices have improved the status of women in society, **radical feminists** believe they have had little impact and that until patriarchy has been removed inequalities such as the gender pay gap will continue. **Marxist feminists** would also be critical of much social policy, arguing that it oppresses women and undervalues their labour in both the workplace and the home.

- Many **Marxists** are critical of government social policies and argue that they can be used by the capitalist system to maintain and justify inequality. For example, they would argue that the minimum wage legitimises exploitation in the labour market while giving the impression that government is acting in the best interests of the low paid. While some Marxists acknowledge that some social policies have benefited the working class, they see the role of sociological research is to highlight the inequalities of capitalism rather than to inform social policy.

- Despite the influence of sociological research on social policy, governments may reject or not make use of research findings for a variety of reasons, particularly cost, their own political standpoint and electoral popularity. Governments' social policies will also be influenced by pressure groups such as the Confederation of British Industry (CBI) and global interests such as the EU.

Exam tip

An exam question may simply ask you to refer to the link between sociology and social policy. In addition to outlining the influence of sociological theory and research on social policy, and factors that act against this influence, you should also refer to the debate as to whether it is the role of sociologists to inform social policy.

Knowledge check 20

What factors may prevent sociological research from influencing a government's social policy?

Summary

After studying this section, you should be aware of the relationship between sociology and social policy. You should be familiar with the following:

- the difference between social problems and sociological problems
- perspectives on social policy and the role of sociology in relation to policy

Questions & Answers

■ How to use this section

Following this introduction, this section of the guide contains four test papers on **Crime and deviance with theory and methods** in the style of the questions you can expect in the A-level Paper 3 examination. The content, timings and mark allocation of these papers are shown below.

Each question is followed by a brief analysis of what to watch out for when answering it (shown by the icon **ⓔ**).

The first two papers include an A*-grade response (Student A) and a C-grade response (Student B) to each question, with commentary (preceded by the icon **ⓔ**). The A*-grade responses represent one way of achieving an A* grade. However, there is no such thing as a perfect essay. An A* grade can be achieved in a number of different ways. The advice below offers some suggestions on how this can be achieved. The third and fourth papers contain an A-Level Paper 3 for you to try yourself after reading the advice.

A-level Paper 3

Crime and deviance with theory and methods

The exam paper is allocated 2 hours.

- **Crime and deviance** Short-answer (4- and 6-mark) questions and extended writing (10 and 30 mark questions). 50 marks
- **Theory and methods** Extended writing (10- and 20-mark questions). 30 marks

Essay-writing template

While there is no set way of writing an essay, the following template can be used to answer the A-level Paper 3 extended writing item-based question 04 on crime and deviance (worth 30 marks) and question 06 on theory and methods (worth 20 marks). The template is referred to in the commentary on the sample answers in this section.

> **Exam tip**
>
> Most of the extended writing questions will make a specific reference to an 'item'. You should always make use of the item but should never copy out material from it. Try to refer to it and use it to make your own point in your own words.

Template for A-level Paper 3 Questions 04 and 06

Introduction — AAA

- **A** — 'As Item A states...'
- **A** — Argument 1 — e.g. the Marxist theory of the causes of crime and deviance
- **A** — Argument 2 — 'However, functionalists argue that...'

Main body

Paragraphs 1–3 on Argument 1 — include AO2 and AO3 points in each paragraph.

For each paragraph, develop AO2 and AO3 by using the following techniques:
- Use studies and examples to illustrate strengths and weaknesses of the argument
- Give specific evaluation points on arguments such as supporting evidence being out of date or that it cannot be generalised easily
- Give evaluation points from different sociological arguments.

Paragraph 4 on Argument 2 — State how it disagrees/agrees with Argument 1.

Paragraph 5 etc. on other possible arguments — State how they disagree/agree with Argument 1.

Conclusion

- 'Perhaps the main strength of Argument 1 is that it is right to point to the importance of...'
- 'Perhaps the main weakness of Argument 1, as Argument 2 points out, is that it ignores the impact of...'

Say something new. Try not to just recap previous points in the conclusion.

The main body of this template is useful for a question that focuses on **evaluating a particular perspective** (such as the Marxist theory). You must clearly apply other arguments showing how and the extent to which they agree or disagree with it. If the question requires you to **evaluate sociological explanations** of an issue or to **evaluate a claim**, you should allocate time more equally to the main arguments.

Depending on the issue raised in the question and the marks available, the number of paragraphs you devote to each argument will vary. As stated, you should not wait until paragraph 4 to use other theories to evaluate; this should be done throughout the essay.

The following typical exam question from Paper 3 illustrates how the template can be used for an essay that requires you to **evaluate a claim** (see page 50 for the item and advice on how to answer the question). You can attempt to write this question using the template under exam conditions. Allow yourself approximately 30 minutes.

Exam tip

A good revision strategy is to practise writing essay questions under exam conditions. Use the template to devise your own more detailed plans for other areas outlined in the Content Guidance section.

Question 06

Applying material from Item C and your own knowledge, evaluate the claim that we are now living in a postmodern society.

(20 marks)

Introduction

As stated in Item C, postmodernists argue that today's society is in fact postmodern: a globalised, media-saturated society in which signs become hyperreal with no reference to society. **Late modernists** argue that while rapid changes have occurred in society they are not the start of a new, postmodern era, instead, it is actually a continuation of modernity itself. However, **modern theories** such as Marxism argue that we are still in the modern era and, as Item C states, there are features of a modern society such as class, ethnicity and gender that have a major impact on people's life chances in society.

Main body

Paragraphs 1 and 2. Outline the key aspects of the modern era and modern theories. Use AO2 and AO3 strategies.

Paragraphs 3 and 4. Outline the postmodern view that we are living in a postmodern society. Use AO2 and AO3 strategies.

Paragraphs 5 and 6. Outline theories of late modernity and how they agree/ disagree with the claim. Use AO2 and AO3 strategies.

Conclusion

Perhaps the main strength of the postmodernist view is that it is clear that factors such as globalisation and the increasing significance of the media in shaping our culture and identity do suggest that we are no longer living in a modern era. For example,...

Perhaps the main weakness of this argument is the Marxist view that traditional sources of identity of the 'modern era', namely class, still exist and that postmodernists ignore the importance of power and inequality in today's society, such as how the ruling class use the media as a tool of ideological domination.

[Something new] A different view is put forward by postmodern Marxists, who agree with postmodernists that we are now living in a postmodern society. However, rather than seeing postmodernity as a fundamental break with the past, they regard it as the product of the most recent stage of capitalism.

Exam tip

In your conclusion, do not just recap what you have already put as this will add nothing to your essay. Also, try to avoid using a 'catch all' point such as 'feminist sociologists would argue that postmodernism is patriarchal'. This is likely to add little as it does not focus on why some feminists would reject the idea of a postmodern society.

Examinable skills

AQA Sociology examination papers are designed to test certain defined skills. These skills are expressed as Assessment Objectives (AOs) and are the same for AS and A-level, though the weighting given to each differs between the two levels. There are three AOs and it is important that you know what these are and what you have to be able to do in an exam to show your ability in each. Further guidance on each of the AOs is given in the guidance and comments. In practice, many answers to questions, particularly those carrying the higher marks, will contain elements of all three AOs.

Assessment objective 1 (AO1)

Demonstrate knowledge and understanding of:
- **sociological theories, concepts and evidence**
- **sociological research methods**

Your exam answers will have to demonstrate clearly to the examiners that your knowledge is accurate and appropriate to the topic being discussed and that you have a clear understanding of it. It is not enough simply to reproduce knowledge learned by rote. You must be able to use this knowledge in a meaningful way to answer the specific question set. This means that you must be able to *select* the appropriate knowledge from everything you know and use only the knowledge that is relevant to, and addresses the issues raised by, the question.

Assessment objective 2 (AO2)

Apply sociological theories, concepts, evidence and research methods to a range of issues.

In certain questions in the exam you will be presented with an item — a short paragraph setting the context for the question that is to follow, and providing you with some information to help answer it. You *must* take this relevant information and use (apply) it in your answer. However, 'applying' the material does not mean simply copying it from the item and leaving it to speak for itself. You will need to show your understanding of the material by doing something with it, such as offering a criticism, explaining something about it, linking it to a particular sociological theory or offering another example of what is being stated or suggested. You will therefore be using your own knowledge to add to the information that you have been given and will be *applying* it appropriately to answer the question.

Assessment objective 3 (AO3)

Analyse and evaluate sociological theories, concepts, evidence and research methods in order to:
- **present arguments**
- **make judgements**
- **draw conclusions**

The skill of *analysis* is shown by breaking something down into its component parts and subjecting them to detailed examination. Analysis is shown by providing answers (depending, of course, on what it is that you are analysing) to questions such as 'who said or who believes this?', 'what does this concept relate to?', 'what does this research method entail?', 'how was this evidence collected?' and so on. The skill of *evaluation* is shown by the ability to identify the strengths and weaknesses or limitations of any sociological material. It is not sufficient, however, simply to list the strengths or limitations of something — you need to be able to say *why* something is considered a strength or otherwise, and sometimes you will need to state *who* claims that this is a strength or weakness. Depending on what it is you are discussing, you may be able to reach a conclusion about the relative merits or otherwise of something, but remember that any conclusions should be based on the rational arguments and solid sociological evidence that you have presented in your answer.

Weighting of assessment objectives

In the exam papers, each AO is given a particular weighting, which indicates its relative importance to the overall mark gained.

Table 1 Weighting for A-level examinations

Assessment objective	Paper 1 (%)	Paper 2 (%)	Paper 3 (%)	Overall weighting (%)
AO1	15	13	16	44
AO2	11	11	9	31
AO3	8	9	8	25
Overall	33.33	33.33	33.33	100

Command words

Ofqual, the body that sets the criteria for all GCE sociology specifications, has an approved list of 'command words' that are used in exam questions. The following are some of the most commonly used, but it is important to remember that the list is not exhaustive, and occasionally other, similar, words or phrases may be used instead. This shows how important it is to take time in an exam and read the questions carefully before you start writing. It is worth learning what is meant by these command words, to ensure that you give an appropriate response.

Define Give the meaning of something

Explain Give purposes or reasons

Using one example, briefly explain Use an example to give a brief account of something

Analyse Separate information into components and identify their characteristics

Evaluate Make judgements from the available evidence

Outline Give the main characteristics

Outline and explain Give the main characteristics and develop these

Applying material from the item Draw on the material provided and develop it using your own knowledge to answer the question. (Remember to make use of the item, but not to copy from it.)

■ Test paper 1

(01) Outline two ways in which the concept of masculinity can be used to explain why males commit more crime than females. (4 marks)

ⓔ You can refer to masculinities related to different social groups such as class and ethnicity. Remember to refer to male crime, not female. It would be helpful to give a brief example of the types of crime committed to illustrate your points.

(02) Outline three ways in which punishments for crimes can be functional for society. (6 marks)

ⓔ To gain full marks, you must clearly show how different types of punishment can be functional. Using a specific example would be a good strategy. As well as justifications for punishments relating to reduction and retribution, responses could refer to different types of justice.

(03) Read Item A below and answer the question that follows.

> **Item A**
>
> Postmodernists argue that we live in a media-saturated society. For many people the media have become the main source of information about crime. Many sociologists have been critical of the way in which the media misrepresents crime, for example through extensive coverage of particular types of crime. Such sociologists have outlined a number of ways in which the media can have a negative impact on the behaviour of some members of their audience.

Applying material from Item A, analyse two ways in which the media can influence crime and deviance. (10 marks)

ⓔ You should spend about 15 minutes on this question. Divide your time fairly equally between each way and write one paragraph on each. There is no need to write a separate introduction or conclusion. You are only required to give two reasons but these must be applied from two points from material in Item A, e.g. media representation of crime, how it impacts on behaviour and news coverage. For each response, remember to quote from the item. You should analyse your reasons in some depth but note that evaluation will also be rewarded.

(04) Read Item B below and answer the question that follows.

> **Item B**
>
> Strain theories argue that crime and deviance occur as a result of people not being able to achieve society's goals by legitimate means. For example, due to a lack of education, the working class may innovate by stealing. Some sociologists also argue that some groups may lack illegitimate as well as legitimate opportunity structures.

Applying material from Item B and your knowledge, evaluate the usefulness of strain and subcultural theories to our understanding crime and deviance. (30 marks)

(e) You should spend about 45 minutes on this question and will find it helpful to use the essay-writing template. Use the first two sentences of the item to help you to introduce Merton's functionalist strain theory. This should be compared and contrasted with the subcultural strain theories of Cohen and Cloward and Ohlin, which are also hinted at in the item. As well as criticisms from other perspectives, you should refer to Miller's version of subcultural theory to evaluate. Rather than simply listing other theories or explanations of crime and deviance, discuss how they have differing views on the causes of 'strain' and of the formation of subcultures — for example, how subcultures are caused by labelling, the neo-Marxist view of 'resistance through rituals' or the New Right's emphasis on an underclass as a form of subculture. Refer also to the existence of subcultures other than working-class boys by referring to feminist or postmodern views and more recent examples of subcultures based on different types of consumption and leisure patterns, such as 'emos'.

(05) Outline and explain two theoretical problems with participant observation. (10 marks)

(e) You should spend about 15 minutes on this question. Divide your time fairly equally between each problem and write one paragraph on each. You can refer to either overt or covert participant observation. There is no need to write a separate introduction or conclusion. Make sure that you refer to theoretical problems such as reliability, representativeness, validity and objectivity rather than practical or ethical issues. You should describe each problem in some detail and use studies to illustrate how the problems may occur in the research process.

(06) Read Item C and answer the question that follows.

Item C

Functionalism is a structural theory that sees society as being based on value consensus. Through institutions such as the family and the education system, individuals are socialised into shared norms and values.

However, some functionalists acknowledge that conflict in society can occur and that some things such as poverty may be dysfunctional for some groups in society. Also, not everyone may share the same norms and values.

Applying material from Item C and your own knowledge, evaluate the usefulness of functionalist approaches in understanding society. (20 marks)

(e) You should spend about 30 minutes on this question and will find it helpful to use the essay-writing template. Make sure that as well as covering evaluation from other theories such as Marxism, interactionism, feminism and postmodernism, you include specific evaluation of the functionalist view, including internal criticisms. Material relating to other perspectives *must* be applied to how they agree or disagree with the functionalist perspectives. You should use topic areas studied, e.g. education, crime and deviance etc. to illustrate the usefulness of the functionalist view. You should also refer to methodological approaches used and contemporary examples.

Student A

(01) ■ Black working-class young males are more likely than other groups to be unemployed and suffer from marginalisation and may turn to a subcultural group to gain alternative status through being 'macho'. This may lead to crimes of violence to demonstrate their masculinity.

■ White working-class boys such as Willis' lads achieved their masculinity through being racist and sexist and resisting teachers' authority. They gained status though adopting an anti-school culture and their behaviour was not only deviant but criminal as they would beat up 'JAs and Pakies' (Jamaican and Pakistani students).

ⓔ 4/4 marks awarded. Two appropriate points are explained with examples.

(02) ■ Deterrence — punishments can help maintain social order by deterring individuals from committing a crime. A punishment like a prison sentence can stop criminals reoffending.

■ Restitution — punishments such as having to pay compensation for a crime can help restore justice and maintain social solidarity.

■ Rehabilitation — prisons can provide education and training programmes to help change the values of criminals. They are aimed at stopping them reoffending.

ⓔ 6/6 marks awarded. Three appropriate points are explained and linked to functions of punishments.

(03) As Item A states, the media misrepresent crime and this can influence crime and deviance through moral panics. News coverage of youth crime for example can lead to what Young called deviancy amplification and can increase levels of criminal behaviour. This was demonstrated in Stan Cohen's classic study on Mods and Rockers where the news coverage of relatively small violent incidents on an Easter Bank Holiday in 1964 were exaggerated and sensationalised. Headlines in newspapers stated that there were '94 Leather Jacket Arrests', but only a small number of youths were actually charged. Through symbols such as 'scooters' and leather jackets the media coverage demonised youth subculture and created what Cohen described as 'folk devils'. This then instils fear into the public thus creating a moral panic about the youth crime. It has been argued that the media coverage actually helped to create these two distinct youth subcultures and created a self-fulfilling prophecy as it predicted more conflict between the groups at future bank holidays. As a result of public fear generated by the media the government may feel pressured to 'do something' about this problem. In the case of a more recent moral panic over the 'raves' of the early 1990s, the government introduced tougher laws and increased policing which may again lead to the deviancy amplification of youth crime. However, postmodernists would argue that the impact of moral panics is no longer applicable today. Increased diversity in news coverage such as 24-hour news means that news stories are unlikely to be reported for long enough to sustain a moral panic.

Questions & Answers

ⓔ This paragraph applies material from the item and has a well-developed account of moral panics with some good analysis and evaluation.

> One way in which the media may misrepresent crime as stated in Item A, is the way the media focus on working-class crime and ignore white-collar and corporate crimes. Marxists would argue that owners deliberately use the media to put across a ruling-class ideology that is pro-capitalist and therefore underrepresents middle-class and corporate crimes. For example, owners such as Rupert Murdoch may set the agenda by deciding to get their journalists and editors to focus on welfare scroungers rather than cover stories about tax evasion, despite the latter costing the country more in financial terms. Similarly the news is unlikely to cover stories that would give capitalism a 'bad press', such as health and safety violations by employers or green crimes committed by multinational corporations. Neo-Marxists would focus on the biased news values of media personnel. Due to their hegemonic culture, journalists are more likely to report on news stories with a pro-capitalist bias. For example, the GUMG has shown how in news coverage of industrial disputes, trade unions have been portrayed by news broadcasts as deviants making 'unreasonable demands' and being involved in 'pointless strikes' damaging the nation, whereas owners are portrayed as making 'reasonable offers'. Due to their shared middle-class culture (the Sutton Trust found that over 50% of journalists went to private or independent schools) media personnel are unlikely to be sympathetic to social problems faced by the working class when reporting on street crime.

ⓔ This paragraph applies material from the item (media representation of crime and news coverage) and there is a good coverage of different Marxist views of causes of the misrepresentation of class-related crime in the media.

ⓔ 10/10 marks awarded.

> (04) As Item B suggests, strain theories are ones which show how the individual responds to having (or not having) the goals and/or the means necessary to achieve the 'American dream' of financial success and how this can lead to deviance. Functionalist Merton saw deviance as being caused by the 'strain to anomie'. Subcultural theories are similar in that sometimes they look at financial attainment but they are different because they sometimes focus on non-utilitarian crime. In addition, instead of looking at the individual's response to strain they look at a collective response. Other sociological theories such as conflict theories reject all types of strain theory as they argue that crime and deviance is socially constructed rather than being caused by the poor values of the working class. Feminists argue that by concentrating on male crimes strain and subcultural theories ignore the issue of gender, such as the increase in girl gangs, and are generally 'malestream' and ignore the reasons why females don't commit crime to the same extent as males.

e A good evaluative introduction which follows the AAA structure suggested in the essay-writing template.

> Merton assumed that almost all people shared the American dream, which was the societal norm. Therefore, those who shared this goal and the institutional means to achieve it were typically middle class and conformists. Such people would view society as meritocratic and for this reason would think that doing well in school (such as progressing on to further and higher education) would garner them the financial attainment they were after, so would not deviate. However, what Merton calls the innovators also had the goals but lacked the means to achieve them and so as a result they created new illegitimate 'means' such as fraud or theft and gained financial reward that way. Merton sees society turning towards anomie (normlessness). For example, the innovator has the goal (American dream) but does not have legitimate means to get it, so they turn to illegitimate means. Therefore, Merton's strain theory is useful in explaining deviance for financial gain because individuals who are innovators have goals but, due to cultural deprivation, lack the skills to legitimately achieve them and so engage in street crime, for example. Merton also outlined three other deviant responses that resulted from the strain to anomie, one of them being the over-socialised ritualist who conformed to the institutional means by working hard and following the rules but had lost sight of the goal of the American dream as they had no interest in career progression.

e This is a reasonable coverage of Merton's strain theory. However, evaluation could be developed with a specific criticism such as there being more than four types of deviance.

> While Cohen agrees with Merton that deviance is a working-class phenomenon, he argues that it is a collective rather than individual response. Working-class boys turn to each other in order to deal with their status frustration. Cohen would also agree with Merton that people do start off with mainstream goals, but would disagree that the only crimes committed are for money. After studying working-class boys in education, he found that, as groups, they experienced a status frustration whereby they failed in their attempts to achieve the mainstream goals (of exam success) and so therefore rejected them. The boys would then engage in non-utilitarian crime such as vandalism of school property as this inverts society's norms of 'education is good' and 'respect of others' property'. This allows the boys to gain an alternative status. As they couldn't achieve status in the mainstream way, they created their own achievement structure. Therefore, Cohen argues working-class boys commit non-utilitarian crime collectively. For example, they would swear at a teacher to gain status from their subcultural group not for financial reward.

e Some good comparative analysis between Merton and Cohen is given here, emphasising the similarities and differences between Merton's strain and subcultural theory based on 'strain'. Again, evaluation could be more developed.

Miller disagrees with Cohen and strain theory by arguing that the lower class do not start off by sharing mainstream values. Miller's view of subcultures is similar to what Merton called 'rebellion' or what Murray describes as an 'underclass' because they have their own distinct values and do not accept mainstream ones. While Miller agrees with Cohen that deviance is caused by working-class subculture, he rejects Cohen's claim that its members are 'frustrated by failure'. Rather Miller argues that the lower class has its own independent subculture based on 'focal concerns' such as 'excitement', illustrated by criminal behaviour such as joyriding. For this reason Miller's explanation of crime and deviance is useful because it demonstrates why groups may commit certain deviant and criminal behaviour such as 'edgework' on the street. However, unlike what Merton would argue, Miller notes that joyriding doesn't happen for money, but occurs due to the desire to achieve their goal of 'excitement'. This means that Miller's explanation is useful for explaining non-utilitarian crime. However, it has been criticised for assuming that those in the 'lower' class who deviate are one homogeneous group and ignoring the fact that the working class may be very different in different areas of the country and that ethnicity may impact on a subcultural group's values.

e This contains some good analysis and evaluation of Miller's version of subcultural theory and his criticism of Merton and subcultural theories based on strain.

Cloward and Ohlin attempt to solve Miller and Cohen's limitation of viewing members of deviant working-class subcultures as one group. They found that deviants are denied legitimate opportunities to achieve success and so form three subcultures. They argue that three different working-class subcultures develop as a result of their differing access to opportunity structures. These are criminal, conflict and retreatist. This is a useful explanation of crime and deviance because it explains why some criminal groups, such as the criminal subculture, work almost like an organisation. They have an illegitimate opportunity structure, which is highly structured in their deviance, e.g. the Mafia. However, an issue is that it doesn't allow someone to be a member of more than one group. For example, a drug user would be categorised as a 'retreatist' as they have 'dropped out' of society but, as South points out, they could also be a member of a 'criminal' subculture if they are involved in selling drugs to feed their habit. Furthermore, it could be argued that these explanations are not that useful in explaining crime and deviance because there could be more than just three subcultural groups. Neo-Marxists such as Hebdige have examined how the working-class youth have developed a range of subcultures to 'resist through rituals' against capitalist society. Cohen and Willis have outlined how the working class have actively used popular culture to reject mainstream values in acts of 'deviancy', such as skinheads wearing Dr Marten boots or Mods customising scooters as part of their youth subculture.

e Cloward and Ohlin's explanation of subcultures is well presented, evaluated and compared to Miller and Cohen. There is some good discussion of neo-Marxist views on the formation of subcultures.

Perhaps the main strength of the strain theory is that it is useful in explaining utilitarian crime, and demonstrating a range of responses that can occur when trying to achieve mainstream goals such as the American dream. However, perhaps the main weakness of Merton's strain theory is that not all crimes are for money. As Cloward and Ohlin acknowledge, not all working-class deviants turn to innovation and utilitarian crime such as theft. Another major weakness of Merton is that he assumes that in the UK we all strive for the American dream, although it could be argued that we are increasingly adopting more Americanised values in Britain as the scenes at shopping centres on 'Black Friday' illustrate. Perhaps the main strength of subcultural theories is their explanation of crime as being a collective response to deviance. However, subcultural theorists fail to recognise that most deviants aren't always part of an identifiable subculture. Interactionists such as Matza argue that individuals will 'drift' in and out of deviance, which strain and subcultural theories don't account for. Perhaps the biggest weakness of both strain and subcultural theories is the Marxist criticism that they are useless in explaining white-collar crime such as corporate fraud, as laws and the definition of 'crime' and 'deviance' are decided by the ruling class to criminalise and control the working class. However, more recently sociologists have attempted to apply the concept of subcultures to white collar and corporate crime such as banking.

e The answer ends with a good conclusion that follows the suggested format outlined in the essay-writing template, addressing strengths and weaknesses of both strain and subcultural theories.

e **27/30 marks awarded.** While there is some good evaluation from different sociological theory, the response would benefit from applying methodological issues such as studying the formation of subcultures via interpretivist methodology. This could be introduced earlier in the main body of the essay and discussed in greater depth. More recent explanations of the formation of subcultures could also be included, such as a reference to youth subcultures based on factors such as 'Nike identities' and different genres of music such as 'emo'.

(05) Perhaps the biggest theoretical problem with both overt and covert participant observation (CPO) is its lack of reliability. Positivists would argue that as it isn't standardised participant observation (PO) is impossible to replicate. They would argue that as a result the method is unscientific as the original study cannot be replicated to see if the findings are true. While CPO studies such as Patrick's study on a Glasgow gang lead to valid data as the researcher gains verstehen, it would be

impossible for another researcher to repeat what Patrick did and get the same results. Although Patrick was a teacher he was young enough to be able to fit in with the gang. Also he has access to the gang through his contact with the gang leader, Tim. It would be extremely difficult for another researcher to gain access in the same way to the gang to repeat the study to test if the findings were accurate. An additional problem is that the dynamics of the group would have been different if a different researcher attempted to study the same gang.

ⓔ A good coverage of the issue of lack of reliability is linked to the positivist perspective and explained with the use of a study.

Despite it being useful to understand the meanings of social groups though the researcher taking part in their activities as interpretivists argue, a second theoretical problem with PO is that it may lack validity. This is particularly an issue for overt participant observation (OPO) due to the Hawthorne effect. As the group being studied know that they are being observed, they may change their behaviour during the activities that the researcher is taking part in. In Punch's study of police in Amsterdam, the officers he spent time with might not have behaved normally. For example, they might not have shown him how they usually treated people during stop and search activities as they might have feared they could get reported for being too aggressive to the public. Similarly, the senior Moonies in Barker's overt study involving PO may not have shown her how they 'brainwashed' new members to stay in the group. In both studies the data may not have been a valid picture of the group's normal behaviour. While CPO doesn't have the problem of the Hawthorne effect, which is why interpretivists prefer it to overt, the fact that the researcher becomes a new member of the group may cause suspicion and change the dynamic of the group, again raising validity problems.

ⓔ Again studies are used well to illustrate the issue of the Hawthorne effect and a lack of validity. There is some good analysis with the comparison between overt and covert participant observation and their lack of validity.

ⓔ 10/10 marks awarded.

(06) As stated in Item C, functionalism is a structural, macro theory which focuses on the needs of society and argues that society is more important than individuals. It is a positivist theory of the 'modern' era, developed by Comte and Durkheim during the political and industrial revolutions of the late nineteenth century. Furthermore, functionalism argues that there is consensus among members of society due to shared values. Marxism is also a macro theory but it rejects the concept of consensus and argues that society is based on conflict. Marxists would also argue that capitalist

society socialises us to accept the values of the dominant ruling class rather than shared values. Functionalists also argue that all parts of society are tightly integrated and have an impact on each other but, as Item C states, even some functionalists recognise that this may not always occur in a positive way. A further criticism comes from interactionists, who reject this macro approach as they want to uncover meanings from individuals and argue that functionalism treats people like 'puppets'.

e The answer begins with a very good, evaluative introduction following the AAA as outlined in the essay-writing template.

Durkheim, a functionalist theorist, believes that there are social facts. He argues that society exists as a separate entity over and above its members and that these social facts shape people's behaviour to serve society's needs. A strength of this argument is that Durkheim was able to show that the suicide rate of Catholics is lower than that of Protestants by using the quantitative method of examining official statistics on suicide. By using a scientific approach of multivariate analysis, Durkheim felt he was able to prove his hypothesis on the social causes of suicide, based on levels of integration and regulation. However, interpretivists would argue that a weakness of this is that by using the positivist approach Durkheim did not uncover the meanings and reasons behind suicide. Durkheim also emphasises the differences between a traditional and a modern society. He argues a traditional society had mechanical solidarity with little division of labour and there was collective conscience which binds everyone together. In a modern society, however, the division of labour promotes differences between groups and weakens social solidarity. In addition, Durkheim came up with the concept of anomie, which refers to a condition where there is a breakdown of social norms. This he felt was one the main causes of suicide in a modern society due to the rapid social change that was occurring. Another strength of Durkheim's views is that in modern society individuals can go into any career path they want to rather than just doing an agricultural job, which supports Durkheim's claim of the division of labour. A further strength is that norms that affect our behaviour do exist in society. For example, we are taught to have manners through primary socialisation. However, Marxists would argue that a weakness of this argument is that modern society has come about as a result of capitalism, which Durkheim fails to recognise. Interactionists argue that this ignores other reasons for suicide which, as stated, cannot be uncovered using a macro, positivist methodology.

e This paragraph provides a good coverage of Durkheim's theory and methodology with some analysis and evaluation.

Parsons developed the functionalist theory of Durkheim by creating the concept of the organic analogy. This means that society is a system where all its parts work together to form a whole, like a human body. Parsons also argues that society exists in a state of equilibrium where if one institution was to break down the rest would be affected. A strength of this argument is that it can be shown in society as, for example, education helps the economy by producing skilled workers. However, a weakness is that, as functionalist Merton argues, not all parts of society depend on each other. This can be shown through the fact that education and the media are only loosely connected and they don't need each other to work. In addition Parsons argues that there is value consensus and social order is achieved by a central value system or shared culture so individuals can cooperate. A strength of this is that there are shared values: for example, in education you are taught to be punctual and the majority of people conform to this. Despite this, Marxists would argue that a weakness of this claim is that not everyone cooperates as there is a lot of conflict. For example, as Willis' study on the 'lads' shows, not all students share the values of the school. Also, these values come from the ruling class and are imposed on people through institutions such as the media. In addition, Parsons argues that society has needs and he refers to this as the AGIL system. One example of this is adaptation, which means that the social system meets material needs through the economy. Another example is integration, which means that different parts of the social system must be integrated to pursue shared goals. This occurs via socialisation by institutions such as education and the media. A strength of this is that material needs and socialisation are important to society. However, interactionists argue that a weakness of this view is that it treats society as something beyond an individual's needs which cannot be negotiated at a micro level.

🅮 The arguments of Parsons are well explained and evaluated. There is some good application of the topic of education to the debate between functionalists and Marxists but the point on the media and individual negotiation could be developed with an example.

Merton is also a functionalist but he points out that a weakness of Parsons' argument is that he is wrong to assume that society is always a smooth-running, well-integrated system. Parsons believes that everything in society performs a positive function but Merton argues that a weakness of this is that some things may be functional for some groups but dysfunctional for others, as stated in the item. For example, poverty is functional for the rich as they gain a greater share of the wealth, but dysfunctional for the poor as they are clearly influenced by poverty in a negative way. However, Marxists would argue that the idea of dysfunction draws attention to the possibility of conflicts of interest in society resulting from power inequalities that allow some groups to benefit at the expense of others, which is a weakness of functionalism. Parsons also argues that all parts of society are integrated and affect each other but Merton argues that a weakness of this is that complex modern societies have many parts that may only be distantly related and may have functional autonomy. For example, a breakdown in the media wouldn't necessarily impact on education.

e The internal criticisms of Merton are well presented and developed with criticisms from a Marxist perspective.

A major weakness of functionalism that Popper would make is that it is unscientific because its claims are not falsifiable through testing. However, a real explanation must identify a cause and we can't explain an institution's existence in terms of an effect in a scientific way. In addition, Marxists argue that a weakness of functionalism is that it cannot explain rapid social change and that the 'shared values' it stresses are actually imposed on us by the dominant class through institutions such as the media and education. Another external critique comes from Wrong, an interactionist, who argues that a weakness of functionalism is that it has a deterministic view of individuals in which they have no free will, which is untrue as people are not puppets and they make their own decisions.

e There are some good criticisms here but they tend to be listed rather than being developed with brief examples.

Perhaps the main strength of the functionalist theory is that there is a central value system, as Parsons argues. For example, everyone in the UK is expected to attend school and the majority of people do conform to this. Perhaps the main weakness of the functionalist theory is that not all parts of society are integrated, as Merton argues, and a change in one part doesn't always affect others. For example, if the media broke down, education wouldn't necessarily be affected. Alternatively, postmodernists argue that a weakness of functionalism is that it is a metanarrative that fails to take account of the diversity and instability in today's society. Furthermore, feminists argue that it fails to recognise the patriarchy that is in society.

e A reasonable conclusion — it attempts to follow the structure outlined in the essay-writing template. However, the example on the media and education is a repeat of an earlier point and the criticisms from postmodernism and feminism could be developed with a brief example.

e 18/20 marks awarded. Overall this essay covers the main functionalist arguments well and there are attempts to evaluate in each paragraph. However, the last two paragraphs need to be developed in terms of adding more discussion to the evaluation points. While the topic of education has been applied to the question, other subject areas, such as crime and deviance, could also be introduced into the debate on the usefulness of the functionalist perspective.

e Total score: 75/80 marks = grade A*

Questions & Answers

Student B

(01) ■ Hegemonic masculinity

■ While middle-class boys conform inside school they may engage in 'youthful high spirits' outside school which shows their oppositional masculinity. For example, they might engage in drinking games and acts of vandalism and sexual offences while on their 'rugger' tour. Middle-class females are unlikely to engage in such 'macho' behaviour to 'prove' themselves.

ⓔ 2/4 marks awarded. While the second point scores marks, the first is a type of masculinity and is not used to explain why males commit more crime than females.

(02) Some kinds of punishment can make it difficult or impossible for people to offend again, meaning the function to society is that further crime is reduced. For example, if you are a thief you cannot carry on stealing if you are put in prison. In the olden days people used to be put in stocks or executed. Another function is that if you have your hands cut off it will be more difficult to commit crime. A last function is that you get retribution or 'payback'.

ⓔ 3/6 marks awarded. The first point on incapacitation scores marks as it is applied with an example. The next two sentences provide further examples of incapacitation so do not score. The third point on retribution is partial as it is not applied to how this is functional to society. It is a better strategy to use bullet points for this type of question as it is likely to be more concise, saving time, and will help focus the response on producing distinct points. If time allows, an additional bullet point could be used as it will be rewarded if any of the previous ones are incorrect (as is the case in Student B's answer to question 02).

(03) The item states that the media can have a negative influence on the audience. Some sociologists would argue that the mass media have a major negative influence on the young and poorly educated because they may have been brought up in broken homes and lack adequate values and are relatively deprived. Through advertising on the TV about the latest gadgets and must-have items, the media could increase the number of thefts and burglaries among the relatively deprived so that they don't feel marginalised for not having the latest goods.

ⓔ This paragraph applies material from the item but lacks development. The point on the influence of advertising on criminal behaviour could be related to the neo-functionalist or Marxist view. Alternatively, the reference to the media highlighting relative deprivation and marginalisation could be linked to the left realist view of Lea and Young.

Another negative influence of the media on the audience is that it may lead to copycat crime. As the hypodermic syringe model argues, the audience are passive and what we see within the media can have a direct effect on how we act and think. For example, in the case of the James Bulger story his death was the result of the two young boys allegedly replicating the events that happened in the film *Child's Play 3*. There have been numerous examples of copycat crime and deviance such as re-enacting schemes from GTA or children slapping each other after watching a Tango advert. However, pluralists would argue that this model is too simplistic in assuming that we are a passive audience. Buckingham argues that even young children are media literate and are able to recognise that a mission from *Call of Duty* is not real life.

ⓔ This paragraph has implicit application of material from Item A. Although it is quite brief, there is reasonable coverage of the issue of copycat crime. There is limited explanation but some good application of examples and evaluation.

ⓔ 5/10 marks awarded.

(04) 'Crime' involves activities which break the law, e.g. theft, and 'deviance' is breaking the norms and values of what is morally expected, e.g. respecting the elderly. The subcultural theorists differ in how they view the relationship of the subculture to the dominant culture.

ⓔ This introduction is too brief. It would benefit from following the AAA approach suggested in the essay-writing template. There is no reference to strain theory and subcultural theory is not explained.

Miller argues that working-class culture is characterised and influenced by 'focal concerns'. He believes that these focal concerns lead the young lower-class people into delinquent behaviour as they over-exaggerate these values. For example, in their peer group there is an emphasis on 'toughness and masculinity', which Miller argues would lead to them committing crimes such as fighting, violent crime and conflict with the law. As these crimes are committed in groups, these values on crime and deviance are passed on to one another. Miller states that this subculture is a response to the nature of working-class life as these focal concerns are a form of 'release' from their 'boring' jobs. However, a criticism of Miller is that he portrays working-class subculture as being completely separate and fails to recognise that a separate subculture like this is unlikely. Also, lower working-class culture is not as homogeneous as Miller suggests.

ⓔ As subcultural theories developed from strain theory, it would be more logical to include Miller after discussing Merton's functionalist view. Miller is better used as an evaluation of other versions of subcultural theory due to his emphasis on the lower class having a distinct culture (compare with the response of Student A). There are some good attempts to evaluate but the last sentence needs developing.

> Merton argues that people engage in deviant behaviour when they cannot achieve socially approved goals by legitimate means. He states that deviance is the result of a strain between the goals a culture encourages individuals to aim for and what the structure of society actually allows them to achieve legitimately. For example, ritualists follow the institutional means (by working hard in their job) but have lost sight of the mainstream cultural goal of the American dream as they do not want promotion. According to Merton, this is deviant as they should be striving for as much financial reward as possible. Merton's goals and means scheme is useful as it shows that there are four different types of deviant response and illustrates that most people are not criminals (most people want material things in society). However, as postmodernists would argue, there are more types of deviant than just four (people are more diverse). Marxists would state that the American dream is only open to a few people, these being the middle class. Feminists would also disagree with Merton and argue that the American dream is patriarchal as it doesn't look at females.

e Some attempts to evaluate are linked to theory but are only stated and could be developed.

> Cohen argues that deviance is a result of lower-class culture and agrees with Merton that deviance is largely a lower-class phenomenon. He puts this down to the fact that the working class develop 'status frustration', which leads them to reject mainstream values and commit deviance. This is due to the inability of the lower class to achieve goals because of inadequate socialisation. Like Merton, Cohen argues that the lower class lack legitimate opportunity structures. For example, the working-class boys he studied failed in education so they used illegitimate opportunity structures to achieve success. In a similar way to Merton's 'innovators', Cohen's working-class boys used illegitimate opportunity structures, such as truanting, to deal with their status frustration. The difference is that while Merton's innovator (such as a drug dealer) is committing utilitarian crime, Cohen's boys were committing acts of deviance to gain status in their group. This shows how Cohen does disagree with Merton, who sees deviance as an individual response to strain, ignoring that much deviance is committed in groups. However, a criticism of Cohen is that he assumes that each generation of lower-class youth develops a delinquent subculture.

e There is some good comparative analysis with Merton but the specific evaluation in the last sentence is unclear and would benefit from being developed.

Cloward and Ohlin argue that there are three different types of subculture: criminal, conflict and retreatist. They state that not only are the legitimate opportunities restricted, but so are the illegitimate opportunity structures. They argue that access to different forms of illegitimate opportunity structures is influenced by the nature of the deviant subculture. The criminal subculture tends to emerge in areas where there is an established pattern of organised adult crime, which concentrates on crime for economic rewards. Organisations such as the Mafia socialise their members into a 'life of crime', which gives them an illegitimate opportunity structure of success. The conflict subculture develops where there is little access to such illegitimate opportunity structures. While they do not gain financial reward, this leads to a group achieving status through gang violence. Finally, the retreatist subculture is formed by those who have failed in the legitimate and illegitimate opportunity structures, e.g. failed criminal and gang members. As a result they 'retreat' into a world of drugs and drop out of society (like Merton's retreatist response). However, a criticism of this is that drug users often have to hustle to feed their habit, so they might be a member of more than one subculture.

e This provides a reasonable outline of Cloward and Ohlin but it is rather descriptive. There is some brief analysis with the different types of access to opportunity structures and comparison to Merton. Again, the evaluation could be developed.

In conclusion, Marxists would argue that crime and deviance helps capitalism and that conflict is based on capitalist ideology, whereas functionalists state that crime and deviance is based on socialisation and creates a value consensus. Durkheim felt that crime was inevitable as in every society some individuals are inadequately socialised and prone to be deviant. However, interactionists argue that crime is based on negotiation and that the key explanation for crime and deviance is labelling.

e This conclusion is not applied to the question and has 'catch all' explanations on crime and deviance from the three main perspectives. Even the section on functionalism is not related to strain theory and so adds little to the response.

e 20/30 marks awarded. Overall there is some good coverage of strain and subcultural theories but the response lacks an evaluative stance in terms of a theoretical debate. As well as needing greater development of evaluation of strain and subcultural theories from different sociological perspectives, the response would benefit from a more structured introduction and conclusion.

Questions & Answers

(05) A major problem with participant observation is that it is not representative as it can only study small-scale groups. It would be impossible for an individual researcher to observe a group much bigger than a class of students. This will lead to a second theoretical issue in that because the sample they use will be unrepresentative the sociologists will not be able to generalise their findings to the wider population. If you just observe one class at a time it is unlikely that you will be able to observe enough lessons to make your results representative of the one school studied, let alone about education in the UK in general.

e **4/10 marks awarded.** This is a brief account which fails to distinguish between overt and covert participant observation. The example given of lesson observations is more likely to refer to non-participant than participant observation. The issue of lack of representativeness is simplistically explained but the point on not being able to generalise findings is a development of this problem rather than being a separate point.

(06) Functionalism is based on the idea of consensus as it sees society as being an agreement among its members. The functionalist theory is widely disputed by sociologists such as Marxists, who believe that society is based on a conflict between the social classes. Functionalism is a macro, structural theory as it focuses on the needs of the social system as a whole. Marxists agree with this approach as it allows sociologists to see the 'big picture' but would criticise functionalists for their inability to explain conflict as a whole.

e The student makes a fair attempt at an evaluative introduction but there is no reference to the item or to criticisms from a micro perspective.

Emile Durkheim developed many of the key concepts for functionalism in the late nineteenth century. Durkheim had noticed a change from traditional society, which he believed to be based on mechanical solidarity (due to little division of labour), to a 'modern society', which he believed to have a complex division of labour. Durkheim was concerned that the strong collective conscience that existed in traditional societies would be eroded by the change to a modern society which gave more individual freedom. Anomie, normlessness, could occur as the old norms and values might be lost in this change, which would threaten social cohesion. Durkheim was a structuralist and saw society as a separate entity of social facts which shape society. An example of this would be Durkheim's study on suicide. Durkheim used quantitative data from official statistics to show patterns, therefore proving that society is governed by social facts. Durkheim found that Catholics had a lower committed suicide rate compared to Protestants. He argued that this was because they were more integrated into society, showing how suicide is caused by social factors.

Macro theorists such as Marxists would agree with this notion that society controls the behaviour of individuals. However, action theorists would argue that this fails to take individual differences into account. Another weakness which could be argued by interpretivists is that all evidence collected was based on coroners' opinions and therefore is not valid. Micro theorists argue that this demonstrates a flaw within the functionalist view of social facts.

e This is a fair discussion of Durkheim. However, a more specific reference to the positivist methodology would improve it. The criticisms from an interpretivist perspective should be developed in terms of the different 'micro' methodology they would adopt to understanding suicide.

Durkheim's ideas were developed in the 1950s by Talcott Parsons, who is seen as the founder of modern functionalist theory. Parsons described society as a biological organism. He developed the AGIL schema to show how four different subsystems in society worked together to ensure society runs smoothly. The idea of the organic analogy can be seen by the way in which certain institutions in society do work together. For example, the education system does have an economic function of providing skilled workers for the economy. It also plays a key role, as Parsons suggests, as being 'society in miniature', acting as the focal socialising agency to ensure that young people are prepared for the world of work. The organic analogy, as it is called, is useful to explain how institutions work together but doesn't explain how some do not.

e Coverage of Parson's subsystems lacks explanation and it would be useful to given an example of institutions that do not work together.

Parsons believes that social order is possible through a central value system of beliefs and goals shared by its members. This is known as the value consensus. A strength of this idea is that there is a lot of agreement in society about values and norms such as basic manners and the importance of basic human rights. However, this idea has been widely criticised by other sociologists, particularly Marxists, who argue that social norms are not shared and agreed upon, but rather forced on to us by the ruling class. For example, we may think a social norm such as punctuality is shared and agreed but this just benefits capitalism as it means that we learn to be punctual workers.

e Here we have basic coverage of the functionalist view of the importance of value consensus with some evaluation from a Marxist perspective. It could be analysed and developed through a discussion of the importance of the role that education, religion or the media play in this process.

Questions & Answers

While accepting the basic views of functionalism, Merton offers an internal critique. He argues three main points against Parsons. First, the idea of indispensability. Parsons argues that everything in society serves a purpose which is indispensable to its existing form. Merton argues that Parsons fails to recognise that not everything in society serves a purpose which is indispensable as there may be functional alternatives. For example, the traditional nuclear family is not 'indispensable' in terms of providing primary socialisation, as lone parents and same sex couples can fulfil this role. Merton also criticises the idea of universal functionalism as not everything in society performs a positive function, as Parsons suggests. Merton uses concepts such as poverty to show that what will have positive actions for one section of society could have negative implications for another. Merton refers to these as dysfunctions. Merton's final criticism of Parsons is the idea of functional unity: that if one aspect is altered, everything else must be too. Merton argues that in modern society there are so many different sections of society that they may be only distantly related. As mentioned earlier, not all institutions in society work together in harmony.

e This is a reasonable discussion of the internal criticisms of Merton. There is some analysis but the last point on functional unity lacks development.

Functionalism is also criticised by other theories. Some people argue that functionalism is not scientific as many of its concepts can be neither proved nor disproved. A main weakness of functionalism is its inability to explain the diversity and instability that exists in today's society. Postmodernists would argue that functionalism ignores individual differences and therefore is not very useful to help understand society today.

e This is a brief and imbalanced conclusion, which does not refer to the strengths of the functionalist perspective. Apart from postmodernism, it does not specifically refer to the other theories that criticise the functionalist view.

e 13/20 marks awarded. Overall some reasonable coverage of Durkheim and Merton, while Parsons is less developed. The response lacks evaluation from other theoretical perspectives such as the micro theories' criticism of the over-deterministic nature of functionalism. While there is a brief reference to Marxism, there is a lack of criticisms from other conflict theories such as feminism. The response also would benefit from referring to theories that have some agreement with functionalist views on various aspects of society, such as subcultural theories of crime and deviance and the New Right views on the family and educational underachievement.

e Total score: 47/80 marks = a high grade C

■Test paper 2

(01) Outline two ways in which crime and behaviour are controlled via surveillance. (4 marks)

ⓔ As well as referring to measures of crime prevention and control, such as those used in prisons, you can also refer to various types of 'liquid surveillance' outlined by Bauman and Lyon, such as in airport security measures or drones. You should outline specific examples of surveillance and these must be linked to control.

(02) Outline three ways in which globalisation has led to new opportunities for committing crime. (6 marks)

ⓔ As well as crimes relating to the global media and technological changes, reference could be made to the emphasis of conflict theories on the increasing range of crimes committed by transnational corporations. Be sure to refer to *new* opportunities of crime and remember that it is useful to give an example to illustrate these crimes.

(03) Read Item A and answer the question that follows.

Item A

Labelling theory adopts a micro, relative approach to deviance; there is no fixed agreement on what is 'normal'. Becker argues that individual agents of social control have the power to label groups such as the working class as deviant. Societal reaction to those publicly labelled will invariably lead to a self-fulfilling prophecy resulting in a 'deviant career'.

Applying material from Item A, analyse two reasons why sociological perspectives would criticise the labelling theory of crime and deviance. (10 marks)

ⓔ You should spend 15 minutes on this question. Divide your time fairly equally between each reason and write one paragraph on each. There is no need to write a separate introduction or conclusion. You are only required to give two reasons but these must be applied from two points from material in Item A, e.g. micro approach, the power to label, societal reaction, self-fulfilling prophecy and deviant career. For each response, remember to quote from the item. You should analyse your reasons in some depth but note that evaluation will also be rewarded.

(04) Read Item B and answer the question that follows.

Item B

According to official statistics, blacks are seven times more likely than whites to be stopped and searched and five times more likely to be in prison. While some sociologists would argue that these patterns are caused by some ethnic groups being more likely to offend than others, conflict theories would argue that they are the result of differential law enforcement.

Applying material from Item B and your knowledge, evaluate the claim that the main reason for ethnic differences in crime rates is institutional racism in the criminal justice system. (30 marks)

Questions & Answers

ⓔ You should spend about 45 minutes on this question and will find it helpful to use the essay-writing template. You should refer to evidence relating to possible racism in the criminal justice system (CJS) from various sources. A good place to start is the item, but you should refer also to evidence from self-report studies. Be sure to look at different aspects of the CJS such as policing and sentencing, as stated in the item, and refer to different ethnic groups. When explaining conflict theories, refer to the various ways the interactionists look at the social construction of crime, such as police labelling, deviancy amplification and moral panics, and refer to Marxist and neo-Marxist views on the causes of selective law enforcement. When looking at the alternative argument, as stated in the item, refer to the different approaches such as functionalists and right realists, who would focus on factors such as inadequate socialisation, and left realists, who point to how members of different ethnic minority groups may commit more crime due to being socially excluded.

(05) **Outline and explain two arguments in favour of the view that sociological perspectives or research should have an influence on social policy.** (10 marks)

ⓔ You should spend about 15 minutes on this question. Divide your time fairly equally between each argument and write one paragraph on each. There is no need to write a separate introduction or conclusion. A good way to structure your two arguments would be to base them on different theoretical views that argue that sociological theory can have a positive influence on social policy, such as liberal feminist, functionalist, social democratic or socialist. Alternative views such as Marxists could be used to evaluate. You could refer to specific policies that have been influenced by sociological theory in your response.

(06) Read Item C and answer the question that follows.

Item C

Positivists argue that by replicating the logic and methods of the natural sciences, sociology can uncover laws of human behaviour. They believe that, like natural scientists, sociologists should use quantitative data to deduce objectively whether a hypothesis is true or false.

However, sociologists from other perspectives have different views, not only on whether this is possible, but on the very nature of science itself.

Applying material from Item C and your own knowledge, evaluate the claim that sociology can and should be a science. (20 marks)

ⓔ You should spend about 30 minutes on this question and will find it helpful to use the essay-writing template. Use the first two sentences of the item to introduce the positivist view on the question. Make sure that you refer to alternative views on the nature of science, such as those of Popper, and the inductive versus deductive debate. As well as evaluation from interpretivists and realists you could also refer to other theories such as feminism and postmodernism. Material relating to all perspectives *must* be applied to how they agree or disagree with the claim and should refer to whether sociology both *can* and *should* be a science.

Student A

(01) ■ The behaviour of prisoners in the panopticon was controlled via surveillance. Even though they did not know for certain that they were being watched, prisoners would stick to their appointed places and would behave, as they knew they might be being watched. Foucault argued that this therefore became a form of self-surveillance. He described this type of surveillance as illustrating disciplinary power, which he felt was spreading to various aspects of our lives.

■ There has been an increased use of surveillance to control illegal immigration. Immigration checks are increasingly using technology such as electronic passports and databases as a means of tightening security.

ⓔ **4/4 marks awarded.** Two appropriate points are explained with examples. It is not necessary, however, to provide the amount of detail given in the first point for this type of question. Up to the end of the second sentence would be sufficient.

(02) ■ Trafficking of women for prostitution has increased since the inclusion of more countries from Eastern Europe into the European Union, which has allowed more freedom of movement between countries.

■ Marxists argue that the growing global market has enabled transnational corporations to commit more green crimes, such as dumping toxic waste in developing countries.

■ Factors such as deregulation on global financial markets have allowed greater insider trading and elite groups have been more easily able to move funds around the world without paying tax.

ⓔ **6/6 marks awarded.** Three appropriate points are explained with examples.

(03) The self-fulfilling prophecy (SFP) as mentioned in Item A is the process whereby labelling is acted upon and carried out. Young demonstrates this process in his study of 'hippy marijuana users'. In the beginning drug use was simply part of their lifestyle. However, aggressive policing led to deviancy amplification of their behaviour, leading to a deviant subculture. This is similar to Lermert's 'secondary deviance', which creates a societal reaction from the labelling process. However, an internal criticism from some social action theorists such as phenomenologists is that labelling theory is too deterministic because it assumes that the SFP is inevitable and the individual has no free choice. In some cases individuals may choose not to deviate further and follow the deviant career. Research in the topic of education has demonstrated that individuals have the power to reject teacher labels of them as deviant pupils. Fuller's study on black girls showed that they rejected teacher labels and formed a pro-education but anti-school subculture. They wanted to achieve and formed study groups independently of teachers, who they saw as racist. Willis' lads also rejected teacher labels as they saw through the myth of meritocracy promoted by teachers and chose to rebel and formed an anti-school subculture. They were able to reject their label and do what they wanted without feeling controlled by their teachers. Becker did acknowledge this criticism and accepted that it was possible for individuals to reject their label. However, he argued that once publicly labelled the pressure to follow a deviant career was often too difficult to escape. The power of social control agencies such as the media would result in the labels such as being a 'druggie' becoming their 'controlling identity', leading to a master status which would be difficult to shake off.

e This paragraph offers a good coverage of the internal criticism of labelling theory with some good application of examples from education and counter-evaluation from Becker.

Marxists argue that a major weakness of labelling theory is that it fails to take into account the wider social context in which labelling takes place. While, as Item A suggests, labelling theory acknowledges that certain individuals have the 'power to label' it doesn't take into account that power operates at a macro level. By focusing on trivial and exotic forms of deviance such as drug taking, labelling theory ignores the fact that labelling and selective law enforcement are a reflection of the inequality and exploitation faced by the working class in a capitalist society. Marxists argue that labelling theory fails to fully explain where the police and media get their labels from. Neo-Marxists such as Hall address this issue by locating the media labelling of black muggers into a wider social context. Hall argues that the moral panic on black muggers was used by the hegemonic culture to control the crisis in capitalism that was occurring at the time. This approach combined a traditional macro Marxist approach with the micro approach of labelling to reach a fully social analysis as advocated by the 'New Criminology' of Taylor, Walton and Young.

e A good discussion of the Marxist critique of labelling theory includes some sophisticated analysis with the reference to the neo-Marxist approaches. As with the first paragraph, a point from the item has been applied to develop a criticism of labelling theory.

e 10/10 marks awarded.

(04) As Item B states, black people are over-represented in prisons in comparison to white people. Conflict theorists such as Neo-Marxists and interactionists would argue that this is because crime rates and official statistics are socially constructed so they stereotype ethnic minorities as more criminal. This supports the argument that the criminal justice system (CJS) is racist. However, functionalists reject this by arguing that ethnic minorities (EMs) do commit more crimes than white people due to their poor values. This shows, they claim, that ethnic differences in crime rates reflect the reality that ethnic groups such as blacks and Asians are more likely to offend.

e A good evaluative introduction, this follows the essay-writing template.

> Interactionists support the argument that ethnic differences in crime rates can be explained by racism in the CJS. Becker would argue that agents of social control such as the police and the judiciary negatively label less powerful groups such as EMs as criminal and as a result they are more likely to appear on police recorded statistics. As well as black people being more harshly treated, as mentioned in the item, this would explain why Asians are three times more likely than white people to be stopped and searched. In addition this label becomes a self-fulfilling prophecy where the labelled person follows a deviant career, which means EMs commit even more crime. Cicourel supports Becker by arguing the police use the idea of a 'typical delinquent' to stereotype EMs as criminal, which means they are over-represented in official statistics. However, while labelling theory is useful to show how deviance is relative, it has been accused of being deterministic as people are able to reject labels and not follow the deviant career.

e While labelling theory is related to ethnicity in terms of differences in stop and search rates, the section on self-fulfilling prophecy and deviant career, and the evaluation of this, is general and not applied specifically to ethnicity.

> Interpretivist sociologists have used observational studies to examine how the police use racial profiling. Holdaway argues that the 'canteen culture' of the police is based on racist stereotyping of black criminals. The MacPherson Report showed how the Metropolitan Police force was institutionally racist in the way it dealt with the case of Stephen Lawrence. However, Waddington's observations of CCTV footage showed that the police stopped and searched on the basis of who was on the streets at night in high crime areas — which happened to be EMs. This evidence supports the demographic explanation of Morris, who argues that official statistics reflect the fact that most crime is committed by young people and EM groups have a higher proportion of young people. However, self-report studies show that whites have a higher rate of offending than black people, supporting the view that the CJS is institutionally racist. Additionally, evidence suggests the judicial process is biased against EMs. Hood found that criminal courts were more likely to give custodial sentences to black males compared to white and evidence also suggests that black and Asian offenders are more likely to be charged rather than cautioned in comparison to white offenders.

e This paragraph gives a good presentation of evidence for and against racism in the police force and judicial system.

Neo-Marxist Gilroy's study of the myth of black criminality supports the argument that the CJS is racist. He claims that the police act on racist stereotypes so that black people appear in greater numbers on official statistics. This explains why, as the item states, black people are more likely to be stopped and searched than white people. Furthermore, he argues that black crime is a form of political resistance against a racist society, as shown by the higher representation of black people in official statistics. However, left realists claim that most crime is intra-ethnic, so most black crime is probably not a backlash against a white society. Lea and Young would also argue that Gilroy is too sympathetic to the black criminal and that crime is a real problem that needs addressing, particularly in working-class urban areas where black people are more likely to live.

🄔 This is a good discussion of Gilroy and evaluation from a left realist perspective.

Hall's study, *Policing the Crisis*, supports the Neo-Marxist view that ethnic differences in crime rates can be explained by racism in the CJS. Hall argues that the police selectively released statistics that suggested that young black males were more likely to be involved in street crime. The resulting moral panic created the folk devil of the 'black mugger', which Hall argues was used as a scapegoat to distract attention away from the 'crisis in capitalism' that took place in the early 1970s with rising unemployment and an economic recession. As a result of this media labelling, the white working class would blame black people for society's problems rather than capitalism. As well as taking on board these racist attitudes, the police were given additional powers to stop and search and use more 'military' style policing. Hall argues that official statistics therefore reflect high levels of black crime due to them being socially constructed by the hegemonic, racist 'control culture' that created this moral panic for ideological reasons. However, Hall's methodology, such as his use of content analysis, has been criticised and it has been suggested that he has not clearly explained how the 'control culture' created this moral panic in the way he suggests. In relation to Asians being more likely to be stopped and searched and appear on the official statistics, this may be due to the moral panic referred to as 'Islamophobia'. As occurred with Hall's moral panic, the police and the judicial system have been given greater powers to crack down on the 'war on terror'. Like left realists, right realists would argue that Gilroy and Hall are too sympathetic to the black criminal. They would suggest that tough, 'zero-tolerance' policing is not institutionally racist and is necessary to control crime in urban areas.

🄔 Hall's study is well applied to the question, as is the example of Islamophobia, ensuring the response does focus on more than one ethnic minority group. There is some good specific evaluation of Hall and evaluation from other theoretical perspectives.

On the other hand, functionalists like Merton argue that EMs lack the opportunity structures to achieve the American dream so they turn to illegitimate means. For example, their poor socialisation means they fail in school so they have to innovate by becoming drug dealers. Similarly, New Right theorists like Murray argue that EMs are part of an underclass who have a dependency culture which leads to crime, resulting from a lack of a male role model. For example, Rastafarian beliefs encourage drug taking. Both of these theories argue, therefore, that ethnic differences in crime rates can be explained by differences in behaviour rather than racism in the CJS.

e This section is rather brief and has limited analysis and no evaluation of the two perspectives mentioned.

Like functionalists and right realists, left realists Lea and Young argue that ethnic differences in statistics reflect real differences. They argue that racism in society means that EMs feel marginalised and socially excluded, due to lack of employment, for example, so they turn to crime to solve their relative deprivation. This shows that ethnic differences in crime rates are explained by the behaviour of EMs themselves. However, unlike right realists, left realists argue that it is society rather than poor values that is the cause of crime. Although left realists do agree with conflict theories that racist policing does occur, this does not explain why blacks are convicted more than Asians. For example, 15% of the prison population is made up of blacks but only 7% is Asian. Marxists argue that selective law enforcement is used to criminalise EMs, which shows the CJS is racist.

e This constitutes a fair discussion of the left realist explanation of why ethnic minorities may commit more crime. While there is a good comparison with other perspectives, analysis on the causes of ethnicity and crime could be more detailed.

Perhaps the main strength of the Neo-Marxist argument that the CJS is racist is that moral panics about EMs do exist, which criminalises them. For example, as well as Islamophobia, since the 1990s there has been a fear about rap music glamorising gun crime among the black community. However, perhaps the main weakness of this argument is that some EMs may simply have different values from white people, as right realists would argue. Ethnic differences in crime rates may therefore be down to behaviour rather than racism in the CJS. Alternatively, subcultural theorists argue that as certain EMs lack opportunity structures this means they seek a collective response and join criminal groups. This further rejects the argument that the CJS is racist. However, such theories fail to explain why only a small proportion of young black males turn to crime and fail to acknowledge that the police themselves have admitted that they are institutionally racist.

e This is a good conclusion, which follows the format suggested in the essay-writing template.

Questions & Answers

ⓔ 28/30 marks awarded. Overall the response gives a good coverage of the conflict theories of interactionist and neo-Marxist theories, which on the whole are well applied to the question, though with some repetition. However, there is a slight imbalance in the essay due to the lack of detail on theories arguing against the essay question, particularly right realist/New Right approaches.

---

(05) Social democrats see sociology as able to have a positive influence on social policy. They share a similar view to positivists and functionalists that sociologists can have an impact on social policies and should investigate social problems and conduct research to make policy recommendations to governments to improve them. However, they adopt a more socialist approach and place an emphasis on the redistribution of wealth from the rich to poor.

Townsend, for example, concluded in his research that there was a need for a fairer benefits system and more public spending on health and education. His research on poverty in the UK challenged the government's official poverty line and instead adopted a more relative approach to defining poverty, i.e. that people should be able to have enough money from benefits to live not just exist. Under his relative measurement there were more people living in poverty in the UK than the government suggested due to the government's poverty line being based on an absolute measurement. As a socialist, and in line with the social democratic perspective, Townsend concluded that the government's social policy on benefits should be changed so that the amount paid to those on income support should be increased to reduce the amount of people living in poverty in society.

However, Townsend's research had very little influence upon social policy, illustrating how, despite trying to be influential, sociological research may be ignored by governments which have a different political agenda. This was also illustrated by the socialist-influenced Black Report's finding and suggestions for social policy on investing in the NHS being ignored by the Thatcher government.

ⓔ This paragraph has a detailed and developed account of the social democratic perspective's view on the importance of sociology to social policy, with some examples and evaluation.

Different feminists have different views on whether sociological perspectives and research should have an influence on social policy. Liberal feminists would suggest that feminist arguments and research in the 1970s and 1980s raised awareness of gender inequality in education and have resulted in governments developing social policies to deal with issues raised. For example, research by feminists such as Stanworth on teacher attitudes and by Lobban on reading schemes has led to governments introducing policies to tackle gender stereotyping in the education system. Much like Marxists, however, radical feminists argue such social policies only serve to legitimise inequality that exists and that they have not addressed the issues of the education system reinforcing and perpetuating masculine hegemony through verbal abuse and double standards.

ⓔ This paragraph on feminism has some good analysis but is less developed and would benefit from the inclusion of specific policies that have been influenced by feminism.

ⓔ 9/10 marks awarded.

(06) As stated in Item C, positivists argue that just as in the natural sciences, sociology can be objective using the inductive approach. 'Can' suggests that it is possible for sociology to be a science, while 'should' suggests that there is a good reason to do so. As there are different views on what science actually is, people have different views on whether sociology can be a science. Positivists argue that sociology can and should be a science by using quantitative methods and verification to establish observable patterns in behaviour and develop causal laws. However, interpretivists argue that sociology can't and shouldn't model itself on natural sciences because human conduct is not governed by external causes but by internal meanings. For interpretivists, the task of sociology is to use qualitative methods to uncover these meanings through verstehen. Alternatively, realists argue that sociology can and should sometimes be a science because, like science, sociology studies unobservable structures as well as observable facts.

ⓔ This is a good introduction, which follows the AAA format in the essay-writing template, and shows good application skills by the use of the words 'can' and 'should' from the question.

Positivists argue that we can and should apply the logic and methods of natural sciences to the study of society so we can solve social problems. They believe that reality exists outside the human mind and society is an objective factual reality which is patterned and can be observed by using quantitative methods. For example, Durkheim used official statistics to discover laws of cause and effect on suicide. He felt patterns in suicide rates were caused by differences in integration and regulation levels. This he discovered by examining correlations in the suicide rates of different countries in a scientific, objective and detached way, just as in experiments in the natural sciences. However, it could be argued that Durkheim wasn't actually very scientific. He did not clearly operationalise concepts such as integration and wasn't completely value free and objective as he chose to study this topic due to a family member committing suicide. Positivists also argue that we can discover laws, like in the natural sciences, on how society works by using inductive reasoning which is verified through research evidence. Furthermore, we should use the experimental method of the natural sciences for research as hypotheses can be tested in a controlled and systematic way. However, interpretivists argue that science doesn't deal with meanings, only laws of cause and effect, so sociology can't be scientific. They argue that they ignore the role played by consciousness, meaning and choice. However, realists argue that sociology can't always be studied in a 'closed' way as it is too large-scale and complex.

e A good account of the positivist approach using Durkheim to illustrate it. It includes some good evaluation of both Durkheim and from other perspectives.

Interpretivists argue that sociology can't and shouldn't be modelled on natural science because this is unsuited to the study of humans and sociology is about internal meanings, not external causes. They argue that natural sciences study matter which has no consciousness while humans do have consciousness and individuals construct their social world through the meanings they give to it. However, positivists reject this and argue that society is an objective factual reality so sociology can be studied in a scientific way. While positivists use quantitative methods, interpretivists favour qualitative methods, which give subjective understanding so we can uncover meanings. Interactionists argue that we can have causal explanations like positivists argue, but through a 'bottom-up' rather than 'top-down' approach. Douglas argues we should uncover social meanings rather than laws. He used a case study approach using qualitative methods to uncover the process of labelling by coroners to reveal the meanings of those who committed suicide. Ethnomethodologists such as Atkinson, however, go even further and argue that we can never know the real rate of suicide, even by using qualitative methods to gain verstehen. Atkinson argues that suicide is an individual act, not a social fact as Durkheim argued, and therefore cannot be explained. Both types of interpretivist approach, however, completely reject the positivist argument that behaviour is determined by external causes and would reject the claim that sociology can and should be a science.

e This paragraph is a very good discussion of the different interpretivist views on the question, with some good analysis using the topic of suicide.

Although positivists see natural sciences as using inductive reasoning, as the item states there are alternative views of science. Popper rejects the positivist view that science is based on verificationism, rather he argues that it should be based on falsificationism. This means a statement is scientific if it is capable of withstanding attempts to falsify it. He also argues that all knowledge is provisional as there is always the possibility that it can be falsified. As Popper argues, seeing one black swan destroys the theory that all swans are white. He believes that some sociology can model itself on natural sciences by producing hypotheses that can be falsified. However, he argues that much of sociology can't be scientific because its theories could not be proved false, such as Marx's view of historical materialism. Although Popper sees scientific communities as critical, Kuhn rejects this as he says that scientists are conformists. They just fit in with the paradigm (shared framework) that they have been socialised into. Kuhn, however, argues that sociology can't be a science because there is no shared paradigm of shared assumptions, principles and methods. He argues that in sociology there are only rival schools of thought, it is not a unified science as there is no shared paradigm. When applied to sociology, Kuhn argues that sociology is divided into competing perspectives, such as Marxism and feminism, so it can't be a science as these disagreements would never be resolved.

ⓔ This is a good presentation of the views of Popper and Kuhn on the nature of science, which are applied to the question.

A third view of science comes from realists, who argue that sociology can and should attempt to model itself on the natural sciences. Realists reject the positivist view that science should only study observable phenomena. Keats and Urry stress that, just like some natural sciences such as meteorology, sociology studies 'open systems' where there is no control over variables and causes are explained by underlying structures that cannot be observed. Realists argue that sociology can be scientific because in the open systems processes are too large and complex to make exact predictions. For example, we can't see patriarchy but it is clear that it impacts on the life chances of women, such as the glass ceiling. However, they also argue that we can't model sociology on the natural sciences because some natural scientists study 'closed systems' under laboratory conditions which doesn't apply within sociology. Realists feel that sociology is similar to natural science because they both attempt to explain the causes of events in terms of underlying structures by observing their effects, which implies that sociology can model itself on the natural sciences. Realists also argue that sociology should try to model itself on the natural sciences as far as possible as this can help study meanings. However, interpretivists argue that meanings are not observable so sociology can't be a science.

ⓔ The realist view of science is discussed well and again is clearly applied to the question.

Perhaps the main strength of the positivist argument that sociology can and should be a science is that Durkheim's study showed that we can discover laws and effects of social phenomena such as suicide. However, interpretivists argue sociology should uncover meanings not laws. Perhaps the main strength of the interpretivist argument that sociology can't and shouldn't be a science is that humans have consciousness while the subject matter of the natural sciences does not. Despite this, positivists argue that society is an objective reality. Perhaps the best argument is the realist view that sociology sometimes can and should model itself on the natural sciences because both natural and social sciences explain causes in terms of underlying structures. Alternatively,

> postmodernists argue that sociology shouldn't be a science because natural science is someone's 'big story' and therefore not the truth. Conversely, feminists argue that sociology should not model itself on the natural sciences because the quest for a single scientific theory is a form of domination because it excludes many groups of women.

ⓔ A good conclusion, which follows the format suggested in the essay-writing template.

ⓔ **20/20 marks awarded.** Overall this response has excellent AO1 on the question and all arguments presented are applied well to the question. The only minor issue is that the postmodernist and feminist views could be introduced earlier in the essay rather than briefly stated at the end of the conclusion.

ⓔ **Total score: 77/80 marks — grade A***

Student B

(01) ■ CCTV

■ Digital finger printing

■ Electronic tagging. This is used as a form of punishment to control the behaviour of offenders, such as those on ASBOs who have curfew times to adhere to.

ⓔ **3/4 marks awarded.** The first two points are partial and would each score only 1 mark as they have not been explained in relation to controlling crime or behaviour. The third point scores 2 marks as tagging is applied to control. This is a good example of the potential benefit of including an additional bullet point, if time permits. This response scores 3 marks rather than 2 as a result of the inclusion of the third point.

(02) ■ Selling illegal goods

■ Human trafficking

■ New global communications have meant that crimes such as identity theft and credit card fraud have increased. For example, fraudsters can send emails globally asking for personal bank details.

ⓔ **3/6 marks awarded.** The first point does not score as it applies to crime in general. The second point is partial as it lacks explanation or an example. The third point scores 2 marks as it has a clear explanation with an example.

(03) Becker believes that once a label has been applied to an individual, it becomes their controlling identity and leads to a 'master status'. This then results in them having a 'deviant career' due to society stigmatising them with a particular label. This forces the outsider to join a subculture similar to themselves. Lemert also talks about primary and secondary deviance. Primary deviance is when the individual does not get publicly labelled and does not see themselves as deviant, whereas secondary deviance is the societal reaction that occurs after being publicly labelled. This links back to Young's study of individuals accepting the self-fulfilling prophecy. Secondary deviance supports Young's idea of deviance amplification, which suggests that when the police try to control deviance, it actually creates more crime and more public concern. However, right realists and functionalists would reject this view and state that it isn't society which creates crime and deviance, but down to a person's poor values. This is a main weakness of labelling theory that it fails to recognise why people commit crime in the first place, before they are even labelled. For example, right realists argue that biological differences between individuals can make some people commit more crimes in comparison to others.

e This paragraph focuses too much on explaining aspects of labelling and leaves the criticism from right realists until the last two sentences. Three references are made to the item: self-fulfilling prophecy, deviant career and being publicly labelled. However, these are not specifically stated as being from Item A.

As Item A states, a key aspect of labelling is that societal reaction is the main cause of deviancy. However, left realists argue that labelling theory is too sympathetic to the criminal and that it does not focus on the deviant act itself. As Akers puts it, labelling theorists seem to suggest the people go around minding their own business when 'wham', big bad society whacks them with a stigmatised label. Left realists argue that labelling theory ignores the fact that crime is a serious problem and that working-class people are the victims of crime, particularly in inner-city areas. Left realists argue that by blaming social control agencies labelling theorists are romanticising the criminal and not acknowledging that people actively make decisions to break the law.

e This criticism of labelling theory from the left realist perspective is clearly explained and a point from the item is applied. However, the discussion is rather brief and could be developed with some more analysis such as what left realists would argue are the cause of deviant acts.

e 6/10 marks awarded.

(04) As Item B states, white people are underrepresented by the criminal justice system (CJS) in comparison to ethnic minorities (EMs). Functionalists argue that higher rates of offending among ethnic minority groups are a result of poor values and socialisation. However, interactionists, such as Cicourel, argue that this is the case due to EMs being portrayed as the typical delinquents by police. EMs such as black people are seven times more likely to be stopped and searched in comparison to white offenders.

e This shows a fair attempt to use AAA as outlined in the essay-writing template. However, the item is being recycled rather than used in the last sentence.

Functionalists argue that poor socialisation and poor values lead EMs to become criminals. Black boys are more likely to come from lone-parent families, where a male role model is missing. As a result, they commit various crimes. Merton would argue that black boys lack opportunity structures. They lack the means to achieve the American dream due to cultural deprivation. However, it may be that these boys did not have the goal of the American dream in the first place. This implies that different crime rates cannot be explained by racism in the CJS. Furthermore, subcultural theorists agree with Merton, that EMs lack opportunity structures. Black boys form subcultures. Miller argues that black boys have focal concerns that are different to mainstream values. For example, they believe in toughness, which could lead to violent crime such as gang fighting. Subcultural theorists say that the CJS is not racist but that EM crime rates in the official stats are accurate.

ⓔ There is some attempt to apply the functionalist view of Merton and the subcultural theory of Miller to the question. However, at times the points lack explanation (such what type of opportunity structures black boys might lack and the types of subcultures black boys might form). The point on lone-parent families and inadequate socialisation could be developed by referring to the New Right view of Murray.

Marxists argue that racism in the CJS is not micro, which is what interactionists suggest, but instead it is macro. Stephen Lawrence's murder in 1999 demonstrates this as the police admitted that they were institutionally racist as they would not have dealt with this case in the same way if he had been white. However, postmodernists would argue that societal values since the 1990s have improved and that there is now a reduction in racism. However, despite this, Marxists still argue that the CJS is racist. Neo-Marxists, such as Gilroy, found that there is a myth of black criminality. Black males are criminalised more than any other ethnic group and therefore appear in official stats more. Gilroy argued black crime was politically motivated as a resistance against the racist society. They are fighting against the British imperialism. Gilroy's approach agrees with the claim of the essay title that the main reason for ethnic differences in crime rates is institutional racism in the CJS. However, left realists Lea and Young argue that their crime is intra-ethnic and not due to racism. Hall found that in the 1970s a moral panic about black muggers was created where black people were used as a scapegoat that social control groups used to distract public attention away from unemployment. However, a criticism of Hall is that he did not explain fully how the moral panic was created and whether people were actually influenced by it in the way that Hall argues.

ℯ The student does not fully explain the difference between the Marxist and internationalist views on the CJS and does not locate these perspectives as conflict theories. There is a fair attempt to apply Gilroy to the question but the potential impact of Hall's moral panic of black muggers on racism and the CJS is not explained. The attempts at evaluation from postmodernism and New Left realism are also not clearly explained.

> Left realists and right realists argue that official stats show real differences in EM offending. Right realists take a conservative view and say that EMs make rational choices to commit crime and are more likely to do this because of biological factors. They argue that the CJS needs to get tough on street crime, which is what black criminals are stereotypically more likely to get involved in, and would agree with the first part of the item and argue that black people's values mean they are more likely to offend. Therefore, right realists would disagree with the claim that their higher crime levels are due to racism in the CJS but is caused by their behaviour.

ℯ The left realist view is just stated. However, there is some application of the right realist view to the question.

> Marxists are correct to argue that selective law enforcement exists and this explains why crime rates of EMs show that the CJS is racist. However, feminists would argue that it ignores gender and ethnic minority crimes such as in blacks and Asians.

ℯ This is a very limited conclusion and lacks balance as it does not refer to the arguments against the essay question. The feminist criticism is very general and the point on Asian crime should be developed in the main body of the essay.

ℯ 18/30 marks awarded. Overall some material is applied and evaluated but the essay lacks any real application of the interactionist and left realist views to the question.

> **(05)** Social problems are issues causing public concern and many sociologists see these problems as areas they should research into and seek to explain them. Sociologists study these as well as other influential factors such as government ideology in order to present practical suggestions for social policies to fix these problems. There are different perspectives on the relationship between sociology and social policies: positivists and functionalists see sociology as providing objective information in order to guide the policy for the good of society. However, Marxists see sociology as having little impact in influencing social policy. They would argue that social policy simply legitimates capitalism and sociological research will simply be used to justify the capitalist society and not expose all of the problems it causes for the working class. The New Right suggest that sociology should suggest social policies to tackle

the culture of dependency. Postmodernists believe that sociology cannot discover objective truth and that all knowledge produced by researchers is uncertain and therefore sociology cannot be used as a strong basis in order to create social policies.

e In this first paragraph a range of theoretical views on the question are presented. However, the Marxist and postmodernist arguments presented here are *against* the essay question and so do not score.

Both positivists and functionalists see the sociologist's role as providing the state with objective and scientific information, by which they discover social problems and practical solutions to them, which can be implemented in the form of social policies. Durkheim and Parsons in their analysis of the education system argued that the purpose of it was to promote a meritocracy which would lead to social cohesion. This is a clear example of how sociology can have an influence on social policy as now education is presented in a meritocratic way, in which anyone can achieve based on their own efforts. This shows what functionalists and positivists believe about the state and how it is set up to serve the interests of society as a whole. They argue that sociologists' research can help produce and implement social policies in order to help society run more smoothly and efficiently. Education policies show that the relationship between sociology and social policy is very close and that sociologists' work can influence social policies. However, government ideology, resources and electoral popularity tend to have a bigger impact on social policies than any sociological perspective.

e The positivist/functionalist view mentioned in the first paragraph is developed here to some extent. However, it lacks reference to a specific social policy on education that could have been influenced by his perspective. The only other argument that is presented in this response is a brief reference to the New Right in the opening paragraph.

e 6/10 marks awarded.

(06) The main method used in the natural sciences is the inductive method where you study phenomena from which you make an observation, then create a hypothesis which you then test. Positivists would argue that you can use this scientific method in order to collect objective facts about society. Interpretivists, however, would disagree and argue that society cannot be studied through science in the same way that rocks and plants are as we cannot uncover meanings of human behaviour using this approach. Realists would argue that we can use natural sciences to study society; however, it needs to be combined with social science to examine underlying structures.

e This is a reasonable introduction. However, there is no reference to the item and the explanation of the realist view is unclear.

Positivists believe that we can apply the logic of sciences in order to gain objective knowledge about society. They argue that quantitative methods such as official statistics should be used within sociology in order to explain social facts. These social facts then create laws about human behaviour within society. They would argue that the job of science is to observe, identify and record patterns such as in lab experiments, which can then be applied to society. Durkheim's study on suicide illustrates how quantitative data can be used to study social facts. He found that suicide rates in Catholic countries were lower than in Protestant countries, showing that suicide is caused by external factors not due to the individual. Positivists also believe in verification in which, after many observations, we can verify a theory and form a law. This supports the use of science in sociology as we can and should produce laws on human behaviour from it. However, interpretivists would criticise methods such as lab experiments as they lack ecological validity and actually cannot be applied to real life situations.

e A reasonable coverage of the positivist approach includes some application to the question, but evaluation from the interpretivist perspective is limited.

Popper would argue that we can never prove that a theory is right, rather he believes in the idea of falsification. He argues that sociology can be scientific as in principle it can produce a hypothesis that is able to be falsified. However, he felt that this was unlikely as much sociology is unscientific and too theoretical so cannot be tested. Popper does, however, believe that untestable ideas can have some value, for example, the Marxist theory of historical materialism — just because this has not happened and is not able to be tested, doesn't necessarily mean it won't be true in the future. Popper argues that science should use the deductive method; that we should draw out hypotheses from an existing theory rather than proving our own theory correct as this will lead to researcher bias.

e There is some analysis of Popper's view of science but this paragraph lacks evaluation and does not compare the deductive with the inductive approach of positivism. There is a lack of application to the question.

Kuhn argues that sociology will never become a science as long as there isn't a shared paradigm in society as we need to agree on what we need to study and how we need to study it. Having a shared paradigm of ideas in sociology is extremely unlikely as theories do not agree with each other on most things. Postmodernists would also argue that a paradigm is not desirable in sociology as it is a biased metanarrative.

e This paragraph is very brief. There is only a limited explanation of what a paradigm is and the point on the postmodern view could be developed.

Interpretivists argue that the scientific method should not be used when studying sociology as human behaviour is not caused by external causes, but internal meanings. Weber argues that we need to uncover meanings behind people's behaviour and gain verstehen by using qualitative methods such as in-depth interviews. Interpretivists would reject the positivist view that you can gain objective knowledge on society through the inductive method as they would argue that research would always include the researcher's values which will be subjective. They would also argue that the main feature of sociology is to uncover social meanings and to gain valid data, not create social laws.

e This is a reasonable, if brief, coverage of the interpretivist approach, which is contrasted with the positivist view of sociology as a science.

Realists, on the other hand, would argue that there is very little difference between the natural and social sciences as both attempt to develop models of underlying structures within society. Realists would also reject the view that science is only concerned with observing phenomena, as positivists would suggest, as many things in the natural sciences like sociology are unobservable.

e This paragraph is very limited and lacks explanation of underlying structures and the realist view on open and closed systems.

Overall, positivists would argue that sociology could model itself on science because we can observe cause and effects within society similarly to how we can in natural sciences. Interpretivists, however, would argue that sociology cannot be modelled on natural sciences because we need to study internal meanings using qualitative methods. People are not solely affected by external causes, but create their own meanings. Realists would argue that sociology can be scientific because, like some aspects of the natural sciences, sociology has to study open systems.

e While there is an attempt at a conclusion this is largely a recap of previous points and there is no discussion of the 'should' aspect of the question. The point on the realist view is new but lacks explanation.

e 11/20 marks awarded. Overall, while this response has a broadly accurate coverage of Popper and the positivist versus interpretivist debate, the response lacks depth, is limited in terms of application, and evaluation is by juxtaposition only. The sections on the postmodern view, realism and Kuhn are very limited.

e Total score: 47/80 marks — a high grade C

■ Test paper 3

(01) Outline two ways in which the state is able to conceal or legitimate its crimes against human rights. (4 marks)

ⓔ As well as referring to factors relating to the power of the state, such as the control of the media or legal system, you could also use the 'techniques of neutralisation' employed by those who work on behalf of the state, as outlined by Cohen.

(02) Outline three limitations of victim surveys in measuring levels of crime. (6 marks)

ⓔ Points such as victim surveys lacking validity or representativeness must be explained in terms of how these do not give an accurate picture of levels of crime. It may be useful to give examples of the types of crime that the surveys are not useful for measuring.

(03) Read Item A below and answer the question that follows.

> **Item A**
>
> Control theorists such as Hirschi argue that people act rationally and generally don't commit crime due to certain 'controls' in their lives. For example, through attachment we are committed to family relationships. Feminists argue that due to patriarchy females are controlled in various areas of society and as a result are less likely than males to commit crime.

Applying material from Item A, analyse two ways in which control theory can be used to explain why females commit less crime than males. (10 marks)

ⓔ You should spend 15 minutes on this question. Divide your time fairly equally between each reason and write one paragraph on each. There is no need to write a separate introduction or conclusion. You are only required to give two reasons but these must be applied from material in Item A, e.g. rational choice, attachment and family relationships, patriarchy in society. You should refer to feminist theories that draw on control theory, such as Carlen and Heidensohn. For each response, remember to quote from the item. You should analyse your reasons in some depth but note that evaluation will also be rewarded.

(04) Read Item B below and answer the question that follows.

> **Item B**
>
> Realist approaches view crime as a real and growing problem and not just a social construction. Right realists argue that due to factors such as the inadequate socialisation of some people, crime, particularly in urban areas, is a serious problem that needs addressing. Left realists, while agreeing that governments need to be tough on crime, argue that social policies should also be tough on the causes of crime.

Applying material from Item B and your knowledge, evaluate the usefulness of realist approaches to crime. (30 marks)

ⓔ You should spend about 45 minutes on this question and will find it helpful to use the essay-writing template, but note that this question requires you to look at two theories. Use the item to introduce the similarities and differences between right and left realists. Then outline and compare the different arguments each has on both the causes of and the solutions to crime. As well as criticisms from other perspectives such as Marxist, interactionist and feminists, you should also give specific evaluation points on both realist arguments. Rather than simply listing other theories or explanations of crime and deviance, discuss how they have differing views on both the causes of and the solutions to crime.

(05) Outline and explain two practical problems of the use of postal questionnaires in sociological research. (10 marks)

ⓔ You should spend about 15 minutes on this question. Divide your time fairly equally between each problem and write one paragraph on each. There is no need to write a separate introduction or conclusion. Remember to focus on the practical problems. Make sure that you refer to the postal aspect rather than problems of questionnaires in general. You should describe each problem in some detail and use studies to illustrate how it may occur in the research process.

(06) Read Item C and answer the question that follows.

Item C

Postmodernists argue that due to the significant changes that have taken place in society, the modern world is dissolving. This, it is claimed, is due to factors such as increased fragmentation and living in a media-saturated society.

However, other sociologists acknowledge that while rapid changes have occurred since the 1970s, factors such as social class inequalities are still significant in today's society.

Applying material from Item C and your own knowledge, evaluate the claim that we are now living in a postmodern society. (20 marks)

ⓔ You should spend about 30 minutes on this question and will find it helpful to refer to the essay-writing template. A good place to start would be to outline the characteristics of the 'modern era' using the item and explain how this has changed with the impact of globalisation. Make sure that as well as evaluation from other theories such as Marxism, functionalism, and late-modern theory and postmodern Marxism, you include specific evaluation of the postmodern view. Material relating to other perspectives *must* be applied to how they agree or disagree with the postmodern view that we are living in a postmodern society. The impact of the media is obviously a key topic area to use to discuss the debate regarding whether we are in a modern, late-modern or postmodern society, but you should also apply other topic areas such as education and crime and deviance. For example, you could discuss how the education system is arguably more diverse now and has moved away from the 'one size fits all' approach of the comprehensive system that existed at the end of the 'modern era' in the 1970s.

■Test paper 4

(01) Outline two criticisms of the use of environmental crime prevention
strategies to reduce crime. *(4 marks)*

e As well as specific criticisms of policies based on the notion of fixing 'broken
windows' and zero-tolerance policing, you could also refer to criticisms from
other perspectives. For example, the left realist view that environmental crime
prevention strategies do not tackle the causes of crime. You could also refer to
criticisms made against the evidence used to support zero-tolerance policies
such as the fall of the crime rate in New York. It may be useful to give an example
of environmental crime prevention strategies to illustrate points. Remember that
with only 4 marks available you should not write at great length.

(02) Outline three reasons why black people may be more likely than those from
other ethnic groups to appear on official crime statistics. *(6 marks)*

e To gain full marks you must clearly link factors such as racism in the CJS
and moral panics involving black muggers to the social construction of crime
statistics. Alternatively, you could link how the criminal behaviour of black
people may be influenced by factors such as relative deprivation and inadequate
socialisation. Remember to refer to black people rather than those from other
ethnic minority groups, and it may be useful to give an example of the types of
crime they are convicted of, such as street crime, to illustrate your points.

(03) Read Item A below and answer the question that follows.

Item A

The increased interconnectedness of societies now means that powerful groups such as transnational companies are more easily able to commit crimes that damage the environment and go beyond national boundaries. This applies to both primary and secondary green crime such as illegal waste dumping. The lack of international law has prompted green criminologists to focus on the harm caused by such crimes rather than simply breaking criminal law.

Applying material from Item A, analyse two ways in which globalisation has
influenced green crime. *(10 marks)*

e You should spend 15 minutes on this question. Divide your time fairly equally
between each reason and write one paragraph on each. There is no need to write
a separate introduction or conclusion. You are only required to give two reasons
but these must be applied from two points from material in Item A, e.g. that
the effects of primary green crimes such as deforestation and air pollution and
secondary green crimes can be borderless. Other points in the item that could be
applied are the references to crimes of the powerful such as governments and
TNCs, the lack of international law and green criminology. For each response,
remember to quote from the item. You should analyse your reasons in some depth
but note that evaluation will also be rewarded.

Questions & Answers

(04) Read Item B below and answer the question that follows.

> **Item B**
>
> For traditional Marxists the very nature of capitalist society causes crime and deviance. The ruling class not only have the power to exploit those from the working class, but are able to make and enforce laws in their own interests. However, neo-Marxist theories generally take a less deterministic approach and some call for a 'fully social theory of deviance'.

Applying material from Item B and your knowledge, evaluate the usefulness of different Marxist theories in understanding crime and deviance. (30 marks)

ⓔ You should spend about 45 minutes on this question, and will find it helpful to use the essay-writing template, but note that you are required to look at a range of Marxist theories. Use the first two sentences of the item to introduce the traditional Marxist view, but do not simply copy the material. As well as outlining how capitalism is criminogenic and uses selective law making and enforcement, as stated in the item, you should also refer to the ideological functions of crime and the law. Use the last line of the item to introduce the neo-Marxist views of Taylor, Walton and Young. This can be developed by a discussion of the attempts to apply the fully social theory by Hall and Gilroy in their neo-Marxist studies of ethnicity and crime. Make sure that you also refer to the criticisms of different Marxist views from other perspectives, including left realists. Rather than simply listing the theories and explanations of crime and deviance offered by other perspectives, discuss how they have different views on the causes of crime and deviance. Also discuss the similarities such as between interactionist theory and Marxism and their emphasis on the law being selectively enforced by powerful agents of social control.

(05) **Outline and explain two advantages of using qualitative sources of data in sociological research.** (10 marks)

ⓔ You should spend about 15 minutes on this question. Divide your time fairly equally between each advantage and write one paragraph on each. There is no need to write a separate introduction or conclusion. You can refer to primary methods such as covert or overt participant observation, unstructured interviews or personal documents. Describe each advantage in some detail and use studies to illustrate each method used. Remember that the question is asking you about the advantages, so do not spend time listing or discussing disadvantages.

(06) Read Item C and answer the question that follows.

> **Item C**
>
> Feminism is a conflict theory that sees society as being divided by gender. Feminists argue that as a result of patriarchy, women are subordinated and oppressed by men. However, different feminist theories have different views on how gender inequality is caused and how women can be liberated from this oppression.

Applying material from Item C and your own knowledge, evaluate the usefulness of feminist approaches to our understanding of the role of women in society today.

(20 marks)

ⓔ You should spend about 30 minutes on this question and will find it helpful to use the essay-writing template, but note that you should refer to a range of feminist theories. Use the item to outline the basic argument of feminist theory before going on to examine the different types. As the item suggests, ensure that the similarities and differences between these approaches are discussed. Make sure that as well as evaluation from some other theories, for example Marxism, functionalism, interactionism and postmodernism, you include specific evaluation of the different feminist views. Material relating to other perspectives *must* be applied to how they agree or disagree with feminist perspectives. You should use the topics you have studied, e.g. education, crime and deviance etc., to illustrate the usefulness of the different types of feminist theories. The methodological approach used by feminists should also be referred to, i.e. its emphasis on using interpretivist methods to gain a subjective understanding of women's viewpoints on various issues of gender inequality in contemporary society.

Knowledge check answers

Knowledge check answers

1 Possible answers include: they ignore female crime and corporate crime; separate subcultures do not exist.

2 Possible answers include: they illustrate how crime statistics can be socially constructed; draw attention to the importance of labelling and its consequences; demonstrate how agents of social control may create more deviance.

3 Possible answers include: they ignore the fact that working-class people are the main victims of working-class crime; they are too sympathetic to the working-class criminal; left realists have described The New Criminology as 'left idealism'.

4 Possible answers include: crime is a real and growing problem that is damaging communities, particularly in urban areas; individualism and the pursuit of self-interest lead to the breakdown of family structure and the community and can lead to crime; labelling and different Marxist theories are too sympathetic towards the working-class criminal.

5 Possible answers include: they are more valid than OCS as they include crimes not reported to the police; they show the 'dark figure of crime'; they have revealed how the 'fear of crime' exists in certain groups.

6 Possible answers include: canteen culture in the police; institutional racism; patterns of police labelling and stop and search; statistics on arrests, cautions, convictions and sentencing.

7 Possible answers include: some self-report studies suggest that women who commit serious offences are not treated more leniently than males; some research suggests that women are not more leniently treated in magistrates' courts, in terms of sexual offences; evidence suggests that the CJS is biased against women; the police now hold less stereotypical attitudes towards females than in the 1950s.

8 Possible answers include: they are not based on old mafia-style fixed hierarchies such as family or religion; they often involve ex-government employees; they can 'franchise' their business to other organisations.

9 Traditional criminology studies patterns and causes of law-breaking, whereas green criminology also examines the harm caused by environmental actions even if no laws are broken.

10 Possible answers include: Schwendinger's definition of human rights is too broad; there is no clear agreement on what counts as a human right.

11 Possible answers include: they are outdated as due to the diversity of new media they are less likely to be sustained in media reporting; the audience are active and are able to see though sensationalist media reporting.

12 Possible answers include: it only works on certain types of crime; displacement; it does not address the causes of crime.

13 This is when those in power achieve social control though the control of the mind (for example, through surveillance and self-surveillance).

14 Possible answers include: victim blaming; fails to examine less visible crimes; fails to take account of structural inequalities; fails to acknowledge that being a victim is socially constructed.

15 Possible answers include: both reject the economic determinism of Marx; they agree that coercion and ideology are used by the ruling class to maintain control.

16 Whereas symbolic interactionism accepts the influence of the social structure, such as the influence of social class on educational achievement or offending, phenomenologists argue that society is not 'real' but socially constructed.

17 Possible answers include: postmodernists are right to draw attention to the inadequacies of modern theories in explaining recent changes in society such as the impact of globalisation; there is greater diversity and choice in society, people are able to 'pick and mix' their own identity via the media and the consumption of cultural products.

18 Whereas the hypothetico-deductive approach of positivism argues that scientific knowledge should be based on verification, Popper argues that it should be based on the process of falsification. Rather than researchers proving their own theory, Popper argues that science should involve disproving the theories of others.

19 Whereas 'value free' means researchers should not let their personal views influence their research, 'value laden' involves sociologists making value judgements: they should be subjective and let their values guide their research.

20 Possible answers include: the cost of implementation; their own political standpoint; electoral popularity; pressure groups; global interests.

Note: Page numbers in **bold** indicate defined terms.

Index

neutralisation techniques 9, 24
New Criminology 12, 13
New Right 9, 18, 19, 47
news values **24**

O

objectivity 45–46
official crime statistics 15–16
opportunity structures 7–8

P

paradigms, Kuhn 44, 45
Parsons, functionalism 19, 32–33
patriarchy 19–20, 38, 39
Perry Pre-school project 28
phenomenology 10, 37
polarisation of the classes **34**
policing 18, 27
positivism
  and science 45
  theory-method link 41–43
  versus interpretivism 43–44
postmodernism 40–41
  feminist 39
  on functionalism 33
  Harvey's neo-Marxism 35–36
  and nature of science 45
  objectivity and values 46
poverty, feminisation of 20
prisons 28–29
punishment of crime 28–29

R

radical feminism 39, 47
realist approaches
  crime and deviance 14–15
  prevention of crime 27–28

views on science 44
recidivism 28, 29
reflexivity **37**, 41
rehabilitation 28
relative deprivation 14
repressive state apparatus 29, 35
reserve army of labour **38**
restitutive justice 29
retributive justice 28–29
right realists 13, 14, 18, 27, 28
risk society, Beck 22, 41

S

science, views on 44–45
selective law enforcement 11, 12, 18, 27
self-fulfilling prophecy 10, 37
sex role theory, Parsons 19
shaming 10
situational crime prevention (SCP) 27, 28
social action theory 36–38
social and community crime prevention (SCCP) 27–28
social construction of crime statistics 15–16
social control 7, 9, 10, 29, 33, 37
socialisation 14, 18, 19, 32, 39
social policy 46–47
sociology as a science 43–45
state crimes 23–24
status frustration **8**
stigmatisation 10
strain 7–8, 9
structural theories 32, 35, 36, 38
structuration theory 37, 38, 41
subcultural theories 8, 9, 12–13

subjectivity, interpretivists 44, 45
suicide 37, 43, 44
Sure Start 27
surplus value **34**
surveillance 30
surveys of crime 15–16
symbolic interactionism (SI)
  labelling theory 9–11, 18, 37
  media and crime 24, 25, 26
  social action theory 36–37

T

theory-method link 41–43
trafficking 22
transnational companies (TNCs) 22–23
typifications **10**, 37

U

utilitarian crime **7**

V

value consensus 32–33
value freedom 45, 46
verification, positivists 43, 45
verstehen, Weber 36
victimisation 30–31
victimisation surveys 15–16

W

white-collar crime 11, 12, 20, 21
working-class
  crime statistics 16
  subcultures 8, 9, 12, 13, 14

Z

zero-tolerance policies 27, 28